The
Cocker Spaniel

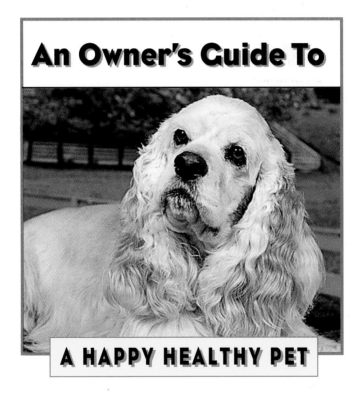

An Owner's Guide To

A HAPPY HEALTHY PET

Howell Book House

Howell Book House
A Simon & Schuster Macmillan Company
1633 Broadway
New York, NY 10019

Library of Congress Cataloging-in-Publication Data
Iby, Judy.
The Cocker Spaniel: an owner's guide to a happy, healthy pet/ by Judy Iby.
p. cm.
Includes bibliographical references.
ISBN: 0-87605-381-9
1. Cocker Spaniels. I. Title.
SF429.9 C55I28   1995
636.7'52—dc20   95-33216
                        CIP
Manufactured in the United States of America
10 9 8 7 6 5

Series Director: Dominique De Vito
Series Assistant Director: Felice Primeau
Book Design: Michele Laseau
Cover Design: Iris Jeromnimon
Illustration: Jeff Yesh
Photography:
  Cover photos: puppy by Pets by Paulette; adult, Mary Bloom
  Courtesy of the American Kennel Club: 21, 23, 25
  Baines Photo, courtesy of Judith Iby: 7
  Mary Bloom: 96, 136, 145
  Paulette Braun/Pets by Paulette: 2–3, 13, 96
  Buckinghamhill American Cocker Spaniels: 148
  Sian Cox: 134
  Dr. Ian Dunbar: 98, 101, 103, 111, 116–117, 122, 123, 127
  Judith Iby: 9, 14, 18, 32, 36, 40, 44, 46, 49, 53, 56, 57, 59, 60, 61, 62, 66, 77, 78, 82
  R. A. Kohl: 8
  Dan Lyons: 96
  Cathy Merrithew: 129
  Liz Palika: 133
  S. & W. Parker: 22, 29
  Janice Raines: 132
  Susan Rezy: 96–97
  Judith Strom: 5, 16, 24, 27, 30, 31, 34–35, 42, 43, 64, 96, 107, 110, 128, 130, 135,
    137, 140, 144, 149, 150
Production Team: Troy Barnes, John Carroll, Jama Carter,
    Kathleen Caulfield, Trudy Coler, Victor Peterson, Terri Sheehan,
    Marvin Van Tiem, Amy DeAngelis and Kathy Iwasaki

Contents

part one

Welcome to the World of the Cocker Spaniel

1 What Is a Cocker Spaniel?   5

2 The Cocker Spaniel's Ancestry   18

3 The World According to the Cocker Spaniel   27

part two

Living with a Cocker Spaniel

4 Bringing Your Cocker Spaniel Home   36

5 Feeding Your Cocker Spaniel   46

6 Grooming Your Cocker Spaniel   56

7 Keeping Your Cocker Spaniel Healthy   64

part three

Enjoying Your Dog

8 Basic Training   98
by Ian Dunbar, Ph.D., MRCVS

9 Getting Active with Your Dog   128
by Bardi McLennan

10 Your Dog and Your Family   136
by Bardi McLennan

11 Your Dog and Your Community   144
by Bardi McLennan

part four

Beyond the Basics

12 Recommended Reading   151

13 Resources   155

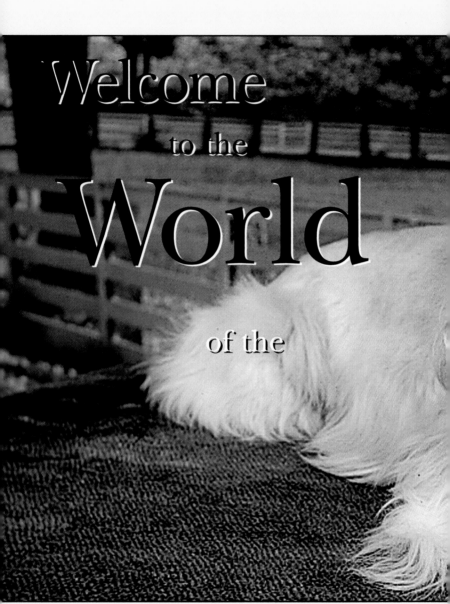

Welcome
to the
World
of the

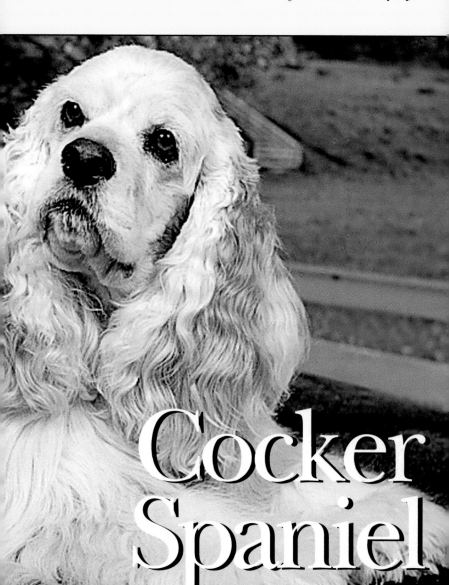

Cocker
Spaniel

External Features of the Cocker Spaniel

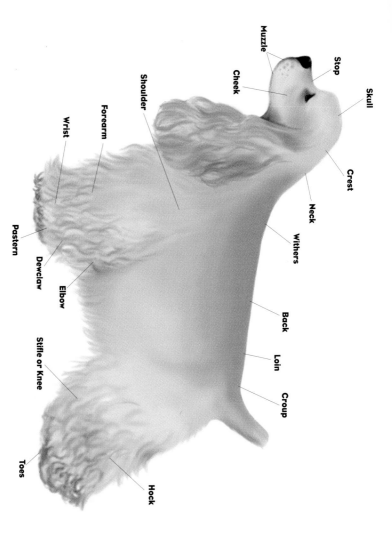

Muzzle

Cheek

Stop

Skull

Crest

Neck

Withers

Shoulder

Forearm

Wrist

Pastern

Dewclaw

Elbow

Back

Loin

Croup

Stifle or Knee

Toes

Hock

chapter 1

What
is a
Cocker Spaniel?

The merry little Cocker Spaniels are the smallest members of the sporting dog family but they possess the biggest hearts. Their happy dispositions and small size make them ideal house dogs. Cocker Spaniels are faithful companions and very family oriented. They thrive on human companionship and will do their utmost to please their family.

Perhaps you are reading this book before buying a Cocker Spaniel. If so, you have taken the first step in the right direction. Perhaps you are replacing a lost Cocker, which speaks for itself. Most Cocker owners would not have any other breed. If you are thinking about acquiring your first Cocker, or a new puppy, I would like to make some recommendations.

Selecting a Puppy

Today's reputable Cocker Spaniel breeder strives for health, conformation, and a sound temperament in a dog. It will be to your benefit to select such a breeder. If you are unsure how to find one, contact the American Kennel Club (see Chapter 13). Another source of information is the secretary for the American Spaniel Club (ASC), Margaret M. Ciezkowski, 846 Old Stevens Creek Road, Martinez, GA 30907-9229. She may be able to give you the names of some ASC members in your area. Other possibilities are the local all-breed kennel club, the Cocker Spaniel specialty club, or your local veterinarian. You could inquire about upcoming dog shows or puppy matches. These are all good places to seek information about Cocker breeders and/or available puppies.

You should buy a puppy from a reputable breeder when you can. An advantage of buying from a reputable breeder is that he or she will be available for guidance as needed. The breeder can be a big help in answering the many questions you'll have regarding your new puppy's upbringing, and can assist you in getting off to a good start with the grooming. Also, you will want to know everything possible about the ancestors in your puppy's pedigree (family tree), and you may even like to hear how the siblings are doing.

A reputable breeder is one who plans his or her breeding. He doesn't breed for the sole purpose of selling puppies for monetary gain. The reputable breeder is proud of his puppies and feels a never-ending sense of responsibility toward them. He doesn't want to add to the list of unwanted dogs waiting to be adopted or

---

WHAT IS A BREED STANDARD?

A breed standard—a detailed description of an individual breed—is meant to portray the *ideal* specimen of that breed. This includes ideal structure, temperament, gait, type—all aspects of the dog. Because the standard describes an ideal specimen, it isn't based on any particular dog. It is a concept against which judges compare actual dogs and breeders strive to produce dogs. At a dog show, the dog that wins is the one that comes closest, in the judge's opinion, to the standard for its breed. Breed standards are written by the breed parent clubs, the national organizations formed to oversee the well-being of the breed. They are voted on and approved by the members of the parent clubs.

euthanized at the animal shelter. The reputable breeder performs the recommended tests on the dogs and breeds responsibly.

The Pedigree

A pedigree filled with numerous champions and obedience titles indicates your dog's ancestors were of sound mind and body, and were trainable. A pedigree that does not contain 40 to 50 percent champions in the first three to four generations should be questioned. On the other hand, a pedigree that contains all champions may not produce the perfect puppy. You will want to examine the pedigree for championship and obedience titles, along with the degree of inbreeding, linebreeding or outcrossing. Ask for health credentials not only on the sire and dam, but on the grandparents as well.

The Standard for the Cocker Spaniel

The pet you have acquired probably has some faults that prevent it from becoming a show dog or potential breeding stock. The breeder is to be commended for

Breeders strive to improve their Cockers with each litter.

placing this dog into a good pet home. Every conscientious breeder tries his best to produce a Cocker that meets the standard, but very few actually make the grade. You may wonder why. It is because of the large gene pool involved. Most breeders select the best candidates from their litters and try to improve the dogs with each litter. Some breeders are successful and others may eventually have to retire an entire line and start over. Regardless, even if your puppy does not meet the standard you should feel confident that he is healthy, and that he will have a good life.

The Cocker Spaniel is probably best known for his beautifully chiseled head and long feathering on the ears, body and legs. Their soft expression and large eyes are never to be forgotten.

Three Varieties

Cocker Spaniels are divided into three varieties based on coat color—ASCOB, black and parti-color. ASCOB is the abbreviation for Any Solid Color Other than Black and includes all shades of buff, chocolate, and chocolate and tan. The black variety includes the colors black, and black and tan. The more common parti-color includes black and white; black, tan, white (tricolor); red and white; chocolate and white; and chocolate, tan and white (chocolate tricolor). The tan points and the red and chocolate color, along with the white in the parti-colors are all recessive colors. This means that both of the parents carry these recessive genes.

A prize-winning Cocker—and proud of it.

You may be lucky enough to acquire a very sound puppy that the breeder is placing with you because his coloring does not meet the standard or the markings are not showy enough to win a prize. Parti-colors are among the hardest to breed for show because the pretty spots may be in the wrong places. The markings on a parti-color dog may make or break the dog. You may acquire a liver-nosed buff or a liver-nosed red and white parti-color. Our standard does not disqualify these dogs, but it does specify that whatever color the nose is, it should be dark.

Coat

People always admire the Cocker's profuse coat, but some grow to dislike it after they own one. The standard penalizes excessive coat. The breeder knows how to cope with too much coat and can trim it out. The pet owner may need to be an accomplished groomer, know one, or be committed to regular shave-downs. Many pet owners are satisfied with regular shave downs. In my opinion, this is far better for the dog than letting the coat grow too long, clump up and get matted. Even so, many pet own-ers take superb care of their Cockers' coats and keep them long and flowing.

You may want to keep this in mind when looking at puppies. Also, you need to be aware that after spaying and neutering, the coat seems to thicken. Therefore, you may want to start out with the easiest coat possible. Frequently the pet owner acquires a truly good Cocker because he is lack-ing in coat and can't win in the show ring.

Size

According to our standard, the ideal height at the shoulders is 14 inches for females and 15 inches for males. It is possible for pet Cockers to range in height from 13 inches to more than 17 inches. Male Cockers over $15\frac{1}{2}$ inches and females over $14\frac{1}{2}$ inches will be disqualified. Males under $14\frac{1}{2}$ inches and females under $13\frac{1}{2}$ inches will be penalized. If you are able to see the sire and dam and perhaps other relatives, you will have a fairly good idea how big your puppy will be when he or she grows up. There is no reference to weight in the standard, but you can expect the 14-inch female to weigh approximately 18 to 22 pounds, and the 15-inch male to weigh about 24 to 28 pounds.

Ch. Triannon Lady Jessica, CDX, TD, owned and loved by the author.

Bite

Many Cockers are placed in pet homes because their bites are off. Bad bites are often the result of retained deciduous ("baby") teeth that should have been pulled. The standard calls for a scissors bite. When the bite is very undershot, the muzzle may not be as pretty. Nevertheless, I do not consider an off bite to be nearly as important as some other faults. I have known dogs that have survived to old age without any problems related to a bad bite.

Attitude

The standard says the Cocker should be "equable in temperament with no suggestion of timidity. Above all, he must be free, merry, sound, well balanced throughout and in action show a keen inclination to work." Unfortunately, there are many Cockers that don't live up to the breeder's high expectations, or meet the standard. If puppies don't receive proper training and socialization this may deter them from reaching their full potential as show dogs, breeding stock and perhaps from functioning as well-adjusted pets. There are certain characteristics that are inherited and perhaps the dog in question just didn't receive the right genes. In my opinion, environment and heredity play equal roles. Nevertheless, I believe most Cockers learn to adjust easily to the good life—the loving home.

Do not pass up a good dog with a minor fault that has all the other qualities you desire.

Revised Standard for the Cocker Spaniel

The Board of Directors of the American Kennel Club has approved the following revised Standard for the Cocker Spaniel as submitted by the American Spaniel Club, Inc.:

GENERAL APPEARANCE

The Cocker Spaniel is the smallest member of the Sporting Group. **He has a sturdy, compact body and a cleanly chiseled and refined head, with the overall dog in complete balance and of ideal size.** He stands well up at the shoulder on straight forelegs with a topline sloping slightly toward strong, moderately bent, muscular quarters. He is a dog capable of considerable speed, combined with great endurance. Above all, he must be free and merry, sound, well balanced throughout and in action show a keen inclination to work. A dog well balanced in all parts is more desirable than a dog with strongly contrasting good points and faults.

SIZE, PROPORTION, SUBSTANCE

Size—The ideal height at the withers for an adult dog is 15 inches and for an adult bitch, 14 inches. Height may vary one half inch above or below this idea. A dog whose height exceeds 15$\frac{1}{2}$ inches or a bitch whose height exceeds 14$\frac{1}{2}$ inches shall be disqualified. An adult dog whose height is less than 14$\frac{1}{2}$ inches and an adult bitch whose height is less than 13$\frac{1}{2}$ inches shall be penalized. Height is determined by a line perpendicular to the ground from the top of the shoulder blades, the dog standing naturally with its forelegs and lower hind legs parallel to the line of measurement. *Proportion*—The measurement from the breast bone to back of thigh is slightly longer than the measurement from the highest point of withers to the ground. The body must be of sufficient length to permit a straight and free stride; the dog never appears long and low.

HEAD

To attain a well proportioned head, which must be in balance with the rest of the dog, it embodies the following: *Expression*—The expression is intelligent, alert, soft and appealing. *Eyes*—Eyeballs are round and full and look directly forward. The shape of the eye rims gives a slightly almond shaped appearance; the eye is not weak or goggled. The color of the iris is dark brown and in general the darker the better. *Ears*—Lobular, long, of fine leather, well feathered, and placed no higher than a line to the lower part of the eye. *Skull*—Rounded but not exaggerated with no tendency toward flatness; the eyebrows are clearly

11

defined with a pronounced stop. The bony structure beneath the eyes is well chiseled with no prominence in the cheeks. The muzzle is broad and deep, with square even jaws. To be in correct balance, the distance from the stop to the tip of the nose is one half the distance from the stop up over the crown to the base of the skull. *Nose*—Of sufficient size to balance the muzzle and foreface, with well developed nostrils typical of a sporting dog. It is black in color in the blacks, black and tans, and black and whites; in other colors it may be brown, liver or black, the darker the better. The color of nose harmonizes with the color of the eye rim. *Lips*—The upper lip is full and of sufficient depth to cover the lower jaw. *Teeth*—Strong and sound, not too small and meet in a scissors bite.

NECK, TOPLINE, BODY

Neck—The neck is sufficiently long to allow the nose to reach the ground easily, muscular and free from pendulous "throatiness." It rises strongly from the shoulders and arches slightly as it tapers to join the head. *Topline*—Sloping slightly toward muscular quarters. *Body*—The chest is deep, its lowest point no higher than the elbows, its front sufficiently wide for adequate heart and lung space, yet not so wide as to interfere with the straight-forward movement of the forelegs. Ribs are deep and well sprung. Back is strong and sloping evenly and slightly downward from the shoulders to the set-on of the docked tail. The docked tail is set on and carried on a line with the topline of the back, or slightly higher; never straight up like a Terrier and never so low as to indicate timidity. When the dog is in motion the tail action is merry.

FOREQUARTERS

The shoulders are well laid back forming an angle with the upper arm of approximately 90 degrees which permits the dog to move his forelegs in an easy manner with forward reach. Shoulders are clean-cut and slop-ing without protru-sion and so set that the upper points of the withers are at an angle which permits a wide spring of rib. When viewed from the side with the forelegs vertical, the elbow is directly below the highest point of the shoulder blade.

The Cocker's ears are "well-feathered," meaning they have lots of hair on them.

Forelegs are parallel, straight, strongly boned and mus-cular and set close to the body well under the scapulae. The pasterns are short and strong. Dewclaws on forelegs may be removed. Feet compact, large, round and firm with horny pads; they turn neither in nor out.

HINDQUARTERS

Hips are wide and quarters well rounded and muscular. When viewed from behind, the hind legs are parallel when in motion and at rest. The hind legs are strongly boned, and muscled with moderate angulation at the stifle and powerful, clearly defined thighs. The stifle is strong and there is no slippage of it in motion or when standing. The hocks are strong and well let down. Dewclaws on hind legs may be removed.

COAT

On the head, short and fine; on the body, medium length, with enough undercoating to give protection.

The ears, chest, abdomen and legs are well feathered, but not so excessively as to hide the Cocker Spaniel's true lines and movement or affect his appearance and function as a moderately coated sporting dog. The texture is most important. The coat is silky, flat or slightly wavy and of a texture which permits easy care. Excessive coat or curly or cottony textured coat shall be severely penalized. Use of electric clippers on the back coat is not desirable. Trimming to enhance the dog's true lines should be done to appear as natural as possible.

COLOR AND MARKINGS

Black Variety—Solid color black to include black with tan points. The black should be jet; shadings of brown or liver in the coat are not desirable. A small amount of white on the chest and/or throat is allowed; white in any other location shall disqualify.

This is a parti-color Cocker.

Any Solid Color Other Than Black (ASCOB)—Any solid color other than black, ranging from the lightest cream to darkest red, including brown and brown with tan points. The color shall be of a uniform shade, but lighter color of the feathering is permissible. A small amount of white on the chest and/or throat is allowed; white in any other location shall disqualify.

Parti-color Variety—Two or more solid well broken colors, one of which must be white; black and white, red and white (the red may range from lightest cream to darkest red), brown and white, and roans, to include any such color combination with tan points. It is preferable that the tan markings be located in the same pattern as for the tan points in the Black and ASCOB varieties. Roans are classified as parti-colors and may be of any of the usual roaning patterns. Primary color which is ninety percent (90%) or more shall disqualify.

Tan Points—The color of the tan may be from the lightest cream to the darkest red and is restricted to ten percent (10%) or less of the color of the specimen; tan markings in excess of that amount shall disqualify. In the case of tan points in the black or ASCOB variety, the markings shall be located as follows:

1. A clear tan spot over each eye;
2. On the sides of the muzzle and on the cheeks;
3. On the underside of the ears;
4. On all feet and/or legs;
5. Under the tail;
6. On the chest, optional; presence or absence shall not be penalized.

Tan markings which are not readily visible or which amount only to traces, shall be penalized. Tan on the muzzle which extends upward, over and joins shall also be penalized. The absence of tan markings in the black or ASCOB variety in any of the specified locations in any otherwise tan-pointed dog shall disqualify.

GAIT

The Cocker Spaniel, thought the smallest of the sporting dogs, possesses a typical sporting dog gait. Prerequisite to good movement is balance between the front and rear assemblies. He drives with strong, powerful rear quarters and is properly constructed in the shoulders and forelegs so that he can reach forward without constriction in a full stride to counterbalance the driving force from the rear. Above all, his gait is coordinated, smooth and effortless. The dog must cover ground with his action; excessive animation should not be mistaken for proper gait.

Welcome to the World of the Cocker Spaniel

TEMPERAMENT

Equable in temperament with no suggestion of timidity.

DISQUALIFICATIONS

Height—Males over $15\,^1/_2$ inches; females over $14\,^1/_2$ inches.

Color and Markings—The aforementioned colors are the only acceptable colors or combination of colors. Any other colors or combination of colors to disqualify.

Black Variety—White markings except on chest and throat.

Any Solid Color Other Than Black Variety—White markings except on chest and throat.

Parti-Color Variety—Primary color ninety percent (90%) or more.

Your purebred Cocker needs love and care to be the best he can be.

Tan Points—1) Tan markings in excess of the percent (10%); 2) Absence of tan markings in Black or ASCOB Variety in any of the specified locations in an otherwise tan-pointed dog.

Approved May 12, 1992
Effective June 30, 1992

AKC Registration

Admittedly your Cocker Spaniel is AKC registered but this fact only states that your dog is purebred. AKC registration tells you little more of your dog's bloodline regarding conformation, inherited problems, etc. However, in the early 1990s, the AKC started recording OFA and CERF numbers on AKC registrations. The Orthopedic Foundation for Animals (OFA) examines hip X rays and grades them so owners know whether their dogs have sound hips or are dysplastic. CERF, the Canine Eye Registration Foundation,

16

records those dogs that physically appear to be free of heritable eye diseases.

You probably purchased your Cocker with the stipulation that it be spayed or neutered. The reputable breeder has a responsibility to refrain from contributing to the overpopulation of dogs. Another important consideration is prior knowledge of a pedigree regarding conformation and health problems. The pet owner is inexperienced and may unknowingly contribute to the breed's problems.

Your breeder may have provided you with a regular AKC registration form or a limited registration form. The regular form may be withheld until you fulfill the obligation of spaying or neutering. The limited registration form entitles you to show your dog in any area other than conformation but no litter can be registered from it. Breeders asked AKC to incorporate this form to curtail irresponsible breeding. If you do intend to breed your Cocker Spaniel, please refer to Chapters 12 and 13 for other reading materials and information.

chapter 2

The
Cocker Spaniel's
Ancestry

The Mayflower and Before

Would you believe that a spaniel arrived in New England after sailing on the Mayflower from Plymouth, England, in 1620? Actually two dogs sailed; the other was a Mastiff. Although spaniels originated in Spain, they were also developed in France and England. In time, they became popular all over Europe before coming to America.

Many sporting breeds, such as the Pointer, Labrador and Flatcoated Retriever, have spaniels in their ancestry. In 1713, Pointers were first imported from Spain into England. Labradors were originally bred from setters and Newfoundlands, and from spaniels and

Newfoundlands. A spaniel-setter crossbreed also helped produce the Flatcoated and Curly Coated Retrievers.

The Cocker today is derived from many types of spaniels from centuries ago. Some of these were called pet spaniels because they were small. They included the Cavalier King Charles Spaniel, the English Toy Spaniel, the black and white Dutch Spaniel, the red and white Italian Spaniel and a straight-coated, web-toed, black water spaniel called the Pyrame. Their colors are visible today in our present Cockers.

Originally, spaniels were bred for hunting game. They were used on land and in the water. It is said that in Spain they worked by running back and forth (quartering) in front of their master, scenting fowl such as partridge and quail, then acted as "crouchers" (setters), downing to the ground. The sportsmen would go over the field with a net, their hawks up in the air, keeping the hiding game close to the ground. The game dared not move or the hawk would get them. In those days, loading guns was time consuming, so the hunter wanted his game to stay put; hence the net. Today, Cockers are to quarter the field, flush game, and bring to hand the downed bird unharmed by their mouths—indicating a "soft mouth." In hunting tests they also make water retrieves.

Later, spaniels were bred as sporting dogs for pleasure-seeking sportsmen, as pets for ladies, and finally as show dogs. Today's Cocker is not only a woman's dog, but a man's dog too. Even though they are the smallest dog in the AKC Sporting Group, their sturdy structure, along with their sporting instincts, make them a hardy little dog. The present Cocker is bred for show and as a companion dog, in which the dog excels. They are true family dogs.

Spaniels have been around for a long, long time. Geoffrey Chaucer mentioned the spaniel (Spaynel) in his writings in the late 1300s. He made it quite clear they were popular even then. William Shakespeare mentioned spaniels in many of his plays.

**FAMOUS
OWNERS
OF
COCKER
SPANIELS**

Lucille
Ball

Elizabeth
Barrett
Browning

Rafael
Palmeiro

Ken
Caminiti

The 1800s

Dog showing began in England in 1859. At that time, spaniels of all varieties were shown together, but eventually they were separated into land and water spaniels.

In about 1870, the Land Spaniels were renamed Field Spaniels, which included Cockers and Springers. They were then divided by weight (under 25 pounds and over 25 pounds) into two varieties—Field and Cocker Spaniels. It was possible for litter mates to be registered as different varieties since size was the only criteria!

In 1891, the American Spaniel Club was formed and their first order of business was to separate Cocker Spaniels from Field Spaniels. At that time, the main differences between the two breeds were weight, height and length of body. A Cocker could weigh between 18 and 28 pounds (which is normal weight today). The field Spaniel was to be proportionately heavier and lower and longer than the Cocker. The latter's weight limitation in the Cocker was replaced by height limits.

The First Registrations

The first dog show in America was held in June 1874. Two black and tan Cockers were shown. In those days, dogs did not have to be registered. In 1879, the first Cocker Spaniel was registered with the National American Kennel Club, which later became the American Kennel Club. The first registered Cocker Spaniel was a liver and white named Captain. Jockey

WHERE DID DOGS COME FROM?

It can be argued that dogs were right there at man's side from the beginning of time. As soon as human beings began to document their existence, the dog was among their drawings and inscriptions. Dogs were not just friends, they served a purpose: There were dogs to hunt birds, pull sleds, herd sheep, burrow after rats—even sit in laps! What your dog was originally bred to do influences the way it behaves. The American Kennel Club recognizes over 140 breeds, and there are hundreds more distinct breeds around the world. To make sense of the breeds, they are grouped according to their size or function. The AKC has seven groups:

1) Sporting, 2) Working,
3) Herding, 4) Hounds,
5) Terriers, 6) Toys,
7) Nonsporting

Can you name a breed from each group? Here's some help: (1) Golden Retriever; (2) Doberman Pinscher; (3) Collie; (4) Beagle; (5) Scottish Terrier; (6) Maltese; and (7) Dalmatian. All modern domestic dogs (*Canis familiaris*) are related, however different they look, and are all descended from *Canis lupus*, the gray wolf.

was the first black and tan to be registered. The first registered black and white, Daffodil, was whelped in 1881. During that same year, the first dark red, Little Miss Rover, the daughter of the immortal Ch. Obo II, was registered. Throughout the 1870s all small Spaniels were registered as Cockers.

Separation of the American and English Cocker Spaniels

The Cocker and the English Cocker owe their heritages to a common ancestor, Ch. Obo, whelped in 1879. Ch. Obo became the founder of the English Cocker. He was bred to Ch. Chloe II, who was shipped to America. In 1882, Ch. Chloe whelped a son, Obo II, who is the progenitor of Cocker Spaniels. Ch. Obo II's conformation does not resemble our present Cockers, or at least it isn't supposed to. In his day, Ch. Obo II was a fine dog. He weighed 22 pounds, but was only 10 inches tall, and 29 inches from nose to the root of his tail.

A 1947 champion, Ch. Adam's Pacemaker.

The American Kennel Club, formed in 1884, separated the Cocker and Field Spaniels in 1905. This had already been accomplished by the English Kennel Club in 1893. Since the beginning of the AKC Stud Book in 1888, there has been no interbreeding in the United States. However, the English Cockers did not receive their own breed status until 1946, thanks to the efforts of Geraldine Rockefeller Dodge. The Cocker Spaniel and the English Cocker Spaniel grew further apart after World War I. The Cocker breeder preferred a shorter-backed, smaller variety and aimed for a more domed head with a shorter, plusher muzzle. The English Cocker is bigger, rangier with a longer

and narrower head, and is narrower in the chest. The
Cocker wears more coat than the English Cocker.

The Proper Name

Only in this country does the name Cocker Spaniel
stand for American Cocker. Outside of this country the
name Cocker refers to the English Cocker Spaniel. A
few years ago the question of renaming the Cocker to
the American Cocker was presented for a vote to the
American Spaniel Club. It was the wish of the membership to continue with the name Cocker Spaniel.

*A family affair:
a Golden
Retriever,
Siamese Cat
and chocolate
Cocker.*

According to English history, the
red-and-whites and the black-
and-whites were more common
than the black Cockers. When
black Cockers appeared, they
were much in demand. During
the early days in this country,
black was supreme in registrations and popularity. Eventually
attitudes regarding the colors
changed and registration increased in black-and-
whites, reds, and red-and-whites. The red-and-whites
had a hard time holding their own against the striking
black-and-whites in the showring.

The Varieties

Cocker Spaniels are divided into varieties, and at shows
each Best of Variety goes on to show in the Sporting
Group. Prior to 1945, the English Cocker was shown as
a separate variety of Cockers. Until the 1940s there had
been three varieties—solid (any solid color including
black), parti-color and the English variety. During the
early 1940s, the solid-color (other than black) Cockers
earned their own variety—ASCOB. Therefore, for a
short period of time there were four varieties of
Cockers being shown.

Until the 1980s, the black-and-tans were moved from
group to group. No variety wanted them. Black-and-
tans started showing with the parti-colors, were cast off

22

to the ASCOB variety, and finally landed where they belonged all along, in the black variety. It is difficult to understand why the black-and-tan dogs were not more readily accepted. Black-and-tans and chocolate-and-tans are very appealing and can be just as lovely as any other Cocker Spaniel. Today they have all come into their own and are readily sought after by breeders and pet owners.

Famous Cockers and Their Owners

In 1921, a black-and-white Cocker, Ch. Midkiff Seductive, made history by going Best in Show at the Westminster Kennel Club show in New York—this country's most prestigious dog show. Her owner was William T. Payne, who proved to be very influential in changing attitudes toward color. It is said that nearly all our partis are descended from the great-great grandparents of this Best in Show winner.

Today it is hard to believe that Mr. Payne owned 350 Cockers that ran loose, when not kenneled, on his 30-acre farm. During those early days, and probably up to World War II, breeding dogs was not only a hobby, but frequently a business. A well-known breeder from that era, O. B. Gilman, acquired the Idahurst kennel in the early 1900s. By today's standards it is hard to believe that the kennel, which was a former residence, housed an average of 125 adult Cockers and puppies, and had a whelping room set up to accommodate 24 bitches whelping simultaneously! The large breeders of those days employed kennel managers and assistants. Frequently the kennel manager was influential in planning breedings. This was not necessarily so for these renowned gentlemen. Remember that Cockers

Ch. My Own Brucie, one of the most popular of all Cockers.

23

were easy "keepers" in those days since they did not sport the coat they have today.

More history was made—and sensational it was in those early dog days—as it would be today. Ch. My Own Brucie "arrived" and went Best in Show, in back-to-back years, at Westminster in 1940 and 1941. Herbert Mellenthin from Poughkeepsie, New York, was the proud owner of this marvelous black son of Red Brucie. Mellenthin and My Own Brucie were inseparable. After the death of Mr. Mellenthin, My Own Brucie was sold to Mr. and Mrs. Peter Garvan for a rumored $10,000. He resided, in luxury, with the Garvans until his premature death at eight years of age. My Own Brucie's obituary was published on the front page of the *New York Evening Sun.*

With the popularity of the breed and extensive breeding practices, it is no wonder that Cockers reached 78,501 AKC registrations in 1947. This number totaled 30 percent of the entire all-breed registrations! In 1994, by comparison, there were 60,888 registrations.

Cocker Spaniels remained in the number-one spot in AKC registrations for over 17 years, from 1936 until the Beagle took over in 1953. They regained the top spot in 1984 and stayed there until the Labrador Retriever moved to number one in 1991. Being on top was a pitfall for the breed. Quite possibly, the worse tragedy that can befall any breed is for it to be popular. It has taken breeders years to overcome the harm done by haphazard breeding. Today, the conscientious breeder takes great pride in raising fewer litters, and emphasizing quality and finding good homes for their dogs.

The Cocker is sniffing for the scent article in an obedience trial.

Today's Cocker

From the beginning of AKC registrations until the early 1930s, the Obo-type dog prevailed—low on leg, long in body, moderate in head and muzzle with feathering on the back of the legs and underside. A "new look" was created in the 1930s. The new Cocker was higher on leg (more up on leg), more compact, and had a shorter muzzle. The feathering was the same as before—on the back of the legs and the underside of the body. Our present day show Cocker began to make its appearance in the mid-1940s. This dog was an even taller, more compact animal, with an accentuated stop, higher dome, a shorter, deeper muzzle, more slope to the topline, and a higher tailset. This Cocker carries a plusher coat—with feathering everywhere, including the front of the legs.

Over the years the standard set forth by the American Spaniel Club has changed many times, with conformation changes in the most recent years. It appears the "die has been cast." Even so, we see all different types of Cockers. Many of these are throwbacks to some of the older types.

*Dungarven
Reddy Teddy
bringing in the
bird in 1951.*

As previously mentioned, the correct, present-day Cocker barely resembles Ch. Obo II, but the inherent instincts are still apparent. Given the opportunity, many of our lovely companion dogs would quickly take off on a hunt. Long ago there was more space and fewer cars. Obviously the world has changed dramatically during the last 50 or more years. It would be foolhardy to allow these little dogs the freedom to run the fields unsupervised. Our Cockers are family to us, and it isn't worth the risk of losing them or having them hit by a car. Nevertheless, a properly trained dog may be able to go out with a conscientious owner.

The obvious is apparent: the Cocker Spaniel was developed in this country. Many well-known breeders have made major contributions to the breed and their dedication has shaped it. In the most recent years there have been at least two breeders who have finished 100 champions, which speaks highly of their breeding programs. Unfortunately, there have been others that have joined the breed for six or seven yards, left their mark, and moved on to another breed.

The Cocker has withstood the test of time and is still favored as a loving companion, as well as being a dog that is able to show off with style in the show ring. The interest in using the dog in hunting has grown over the last decade. This instinct has been carried over the centuries. The Cocker Spaniel is easily trained and enjoys performing in obedience. In summary, I would have to say its most important function is to be a good ambassador and please one and all.

chapter 3

The **World**

According to the
Cocker Spaniel

Most Cocker Spaniels are merry little dogs that fit into every environment. Their tails never stop wagging as they strive for human companionship and attention.

Originally, Cockers were bred and used as hunting dogs. Even though their conformation has greatly changed, their hunting instinct has not. Breeders and many others continue to prove that these dogs have not lost their hunting ability.

The Cocker Spaniel has a keen nose. Owners tell stories about their dogs trying to get at the lost toy

under the sofa (which was lost days before), or sitting faithfully by the tall bookcase where the toy is on a high shelf and out of sight. Because of the Cocker's excellent scenting ability, it has even been used to search for drugs at airports.

The Versatile Cocker

Cockers are intelligent and are quick learners. Sometimes they can even be considered a little stubborn, because it can take time to undo something they have learned incorrectly. Cockers are able performers in the obedience ring, and love the new sport of agility. Agility tests are confidence builders as well as a lot of fun. They even seem to remove stress.

Cockers can easily be trained for hunting and tracking. Both of these sports enable the dog and handler to get some much-needed exercise and enjoy nature. There is nothing more rewarding than watching the Cocker use its nose. My dogs in full coat have gone out into the field and have worked for me in rain and snow. They have returned looking like drowned rats, but they were happy. Over the years, I have found obedience and tracking to be most rewarding. I have dabbled in hunting and agility but just couldn't find time for everything. Through these sports you have the opportunity to meet many wonderful people who share a common interest—dogs. (For more on these activities, see Chapter 9.)

Understanding Your Cocker

Dogs of all breeds exhibit several kinds of behavior. For instance, there is the scared puppy that may eventually grow into the dog that bites out of fear. Other dogs may be somewhat reserved and aloof, and

---

A DOG'S SENSES

Sight: With their eyes located farther apart than ours, dogs can detect movement at a greater distance than we can, but they can't see as well up close. They can also see better in less light, but can't distinguish many colors.

Sound: Dogs can hear about four times better than we can, and they can hear high-pitched sounds especially well. Their ancestors, the wolves, howled to let other wolves know where they were; our dogs do the same, but they have a wider range of vocalizations, including barks, whimpers, moans and whines.

Smell: A dog's nose is his greatest sensory organ. His sense of smell is so great he can follow a trail that's weeks old, detect odors diluted to one-millionth the concentration we'd need to notice them, even sniff out a person under water!

Taste: Dogs have fewer taste buds than we do, so they're likelier to try anything—and usually do, which is why it's especially important for their owners to monitor their food intake. Dogs are omnivores, which means they eat meat as well as vegetable matter like grasses and weeds.

Touch: Dogs are social animals and love to be petted, groomed and played with.

---

friendship shouldn't be forced upon them. Both of these types of dogs need to be allowed to make friends on their own terms—let the dog approach the stranger.

Another type is the dominant dog who intimidates its owner. This is particularly bad for a first-time dog owner. It is amazing how many people are dominated by their puppies. I have often noticed that the nicest people frequently own the worst-behaved dogs. Their dogs are spoiled and take advantage of them. The own-ers do not know how to correctly discipline their dogs. That's why training classes are so important for you and your Cocker. (See Chapter 8 for more on training.)

If your dog exhibits aggressive behavior, you need to consult a specialist in canine behavior. Obedience training will help establish you as the Alpha figure, but this may not be enough. Do not procrastinate. Shaking or other physical punishment may not be appropriate for your dog and usually makes the problem worse. Some dogs with behavior problems won't tolerate eye contact. It is best never to play tug-of-war with your puppy, as this can encourage aggressive behavior.

It's easy to see why Cockers are such lovable dogs.

Cocker Characteristics

Over the years, some Cockers have given the breed a bad reputation. Cockers are very intelligent and some, if given the opportunity, will quickly intimidate the meek. Because of their past experiences, some veteri-narians are suspicious of them. Today there are any number of breeds that exhibit the same poor behavior for which the Cocker was once blamed. Cockers' tem-peraments have greatly improved; we seldom see aggressive dogs, though occasionally we see fearful ones. These dogs usually behave very well around their owners, but are afraid of strangers and new environments. Again, obedience training and socializing will establish confidence.

I have found some of my Cockers to be unusually perceptive. These dogs are utterly amazing, as they notice any changes around the house. Some of them act as if you had intentionally set a booby trap when all you did

was move something to a different spot or bring home a bag of groceries. Dogs can really be amusing. Usually they only act this way in their home environment since they know where everything belongs.

Cockers are excellent swimmers, although mine were afraid to take the initial plunge. I taught them to swim by taking them into the water on a nylon buckle, or harness and leash. In this way, I had control over them so they wouldn't get into trouble. We would go far enough so they had to swim. A beginner will be fright-

Cockers are intelligent and adaptable.

ened, if not frantic, and will try to dog paddle with his head and front legs coming up. By giving the dog a stick, canvas dummy or some other buoyant object, he will keep his head at the water line. This helps the dog learn to swim.

I do warn you that once a dog has been in the water, he may go in more often than you like. This is especially true with the swimming pool. Cockers have been known to dive in during inclement weather. If you do have a swimming pool, make sure your dog is always supervised while in the yard. Dogs have drowned because they couldn't get out.

A word of advice: If you do allow your dog to swim, you need to apply a drying agent to the ears after he is out of the water. Also, you need to dry the dog off after his swim.

Toys and Other Objects

Some Cockers are natural retrievers, while others could care less. At one time I owned a Labrador and it was a little tiring collecting all the "no-no" items (especially those off the kitchen counter) that she had retrieved from around the house. Along that same line, there are Cockers who will always pick up socks and other miscellaneous items and carry them around. Because there's always the danger your dog could eat a sock or other small object, it is best to keep these "goodies"

Like all dogs, Cockers love to be pampered.

out of her reach. One of my dogs used to take great delight in parading the laundry in front of company. I was embarrassed more than once.

Some dogs go bananas over toys. Small toys can be easily swallowed so watch over and account for them. These same dogs may not give up until they "kill" the squeaky mechanism, which can be quickly ingested. If ever your dog has a tiny object that needs to be taken away, don't threaten the dog by trying to take it. It would be better to distract her away from the object. Some dogs may be inclined to quickly swallow the object rather than give it up.

CHARACTERISTICS OF THE COCKER SPANIEL

Merry

Keen sense of smell

Very intelligent

Highly perceptive

Inquisitive

At the veterinary clinic where I work, we do not recommend giving rawhides of any kind. If for no other reason than that they can lead to gastrointestinal upsets; they can also cause blockage in the intestinal tract and require surgery.

Safe toys are those made of hard plastic, or rope bones. Because Cockers are susceptible to back problems, be careful not to overdo games involving running, jumping and twisting, which can exacerbate this condition.

Sandor's Pride and Joy, CDX, CGC, strutting her stuff in agility.

Toys are a wonderful way of communicating with your dog. Frequently the dog retrieves a toy and brings it back to you for more retrieves. This is her way of asking for attention. Squeaking a squeaky toy is a good way of getting your dog's attention or getting her to come to you.

MORE INFORMATION ON COCKER SPANIELS

NATIONAL BREED CLUB

The American Spaniel Club
Mrs. Margaret M. Ciezkowski, Secretary
846 Old Stevens Creek Road
Martinez, GA 30907-9227

The club can give you information on all aspects of the breed, including breed, obedience and hunting clubs in your area. Inquire about membership.

BOOKS

Alton, Lloyd & Gorodner, Bill. *The World of the Cocker Spaniel.* Neptune, N.J.: TFH Publications, 1994.

Austin, Norman A. *The Complete American Cocker Spaniel.* New York: Howell Book House, 1993.

Brearly, Joan McDonald. *The Book of the Cocker Spaniel.* Neptune, N.J.: TFH Publications, 1980.

Grossman, Dr. Alvin. *The American Cocker Spaniel,* Wilsonville, Ore.: Doral Publications, 1988.

Sucher, Jamie. *Cocker Spaniels, A Complete Pet Owner's Manual.* Hauppauge, N.Y.: Barron's Educational Series, 1993.

MAGAZINES

The American Cocker Magazine, 14531 Jefferson Street, Midway City, CA 92655.

The Cocker Spaniel Leader, 9700 Jersey Mill Road, NW, Pataskala, OH 43062-9750.

VIDEOS

American Kennel Club. *Cocker Spaniels.*

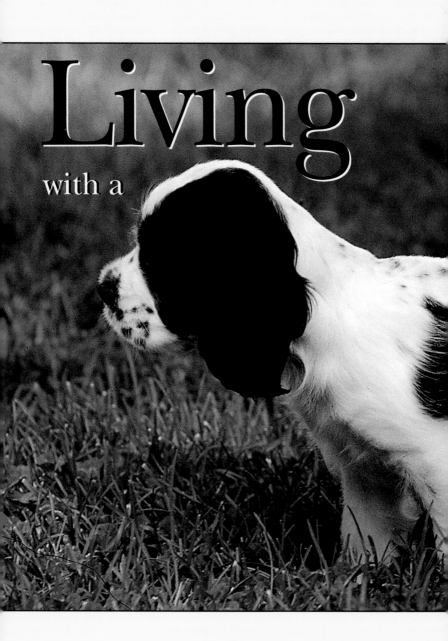

Living

with a

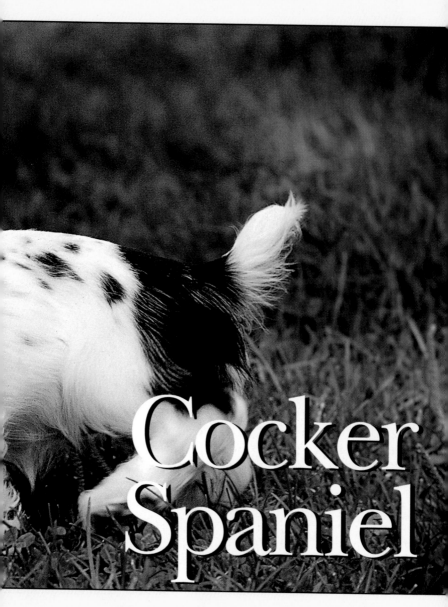

Cocker Spaniel

chapter 4

Bringing your
Cocker Spaniel
Home

Congratulations! You are about to start on a wonderful adventure. I envy you. I have owned numerous Cocker Spaniels, but I am thrilled each time I acquire a new one. Not only are Cocker Spaniels devoted and delightful, but they are eager to learn. Each and every one of them is endearing with his own personality.

House and Crate Training

Obviously, and rightly so, housetraining is one of your major concerns. An important point is that it is easiest to housetrain healthy, worm-free dogs that eat a premium diet without variations.

I am not a believer in scolding the puppy for accidents unless I catch him in the process. Scolding can encourage submissiveness, which may already be an inherent problem in the Cocker. It is far better to prevent accidents: You must learn to anticipate your puppy's needs. It takes some effort on your part, but can be accomplished in a relatively short time. Read on.

CRATE TRAINING

I was introduced to the crate concept in 1970, and it has been a lifesaver. All puppies learn to crate train easily and this simplifies housetraining. Not only does the crate aid in housetraining, but it provides the safest environment for your puppy. Eventually your puppy will look at the crate as his den, his own special place where he can enjoy peace and quiet. Don't be surprised if your puppy hoards his toys or other objects in the crate.

There are two basic types of crates: fiberglass and metal. Fiberglass crates are usually less expensive than metal ones and are easily cleaned. They are the safer of the two, particularly in the car during travel. Metal crates are a little noisier, but they allow more air flow. They also allow the puppy to see more, which makes some puppies happier. There are some precautions you should take with the metal crates. While a dog should never be left in any crate with a collar on, this is especially true with the metal crate. There is always the occasional puppy that will work the top or side loose on the metal crate and then get its head caught. If your puppy's middle name is "Houdini," use snaps to secure the top and sides of the crate.

Eight weeks is a good age physically and mentally for the puppy to start housetraining. However, weather permitting, I introduce my six-week-old puppies to the great outdoors. I want them to get used to going potty outside. Do not use newspaper as a substitute. It is a difficult habit to break. Newspaper-trained dogs are

PUPPY ESSENTIALS

Your new puppy will need:

food bowl

water bowl

collar

leash

I. D. tag

bed

crate

toys

grooming supplies

more interested in "going" on paper than outside where they belong.

Young puppies urinate frequently, but usually they learn to hold it for longer periods of time when they are crated. This is another advantage of the crate. Some very young puppies need to go every 15 to 30 minutes while they are playing in the house. Usually you will notice them start to circle or wander off looking for a spot. Playing in the house should never be allowed unless it is under direct supervision. *Never, and I mean never,* give a puppy freedom in the house unless his housetraining is reliable.

USING THE CRATE

When using a crate you must remember to exercise the puppy any time he is removed from the crate. Otherwise the puppy could get excited with his freedom and have an accident. It is best to take the young puppy out as soon as you get up, and of course, before bedtime or before crating if you are leaving the house for a long period of time. During the day you will need to take the puppy out after every meal and every 15 to 30 minutes during playtime. When you are at home, a younger puppy needs to go out more frequently. Usually they will whine and let you know it's time.

A crate gives your puppy a safe place that's all hers.

If possible, it is best to confine the puppy or untrained dog to a fairly small crate. After he is trained, you can give him a larger crate if he is to be confined for long periods of time. The reason for starting with a small crate is that dogs do not like to soil their own area. When using a larger crate, the puppy could use one end to potty, the other end to sleep, and still keep himself clean. I do not recommend putting any bedding in the crate. If the puppy urinates, the bedding will absorb it and the puppy will keep himself clean. Also puppies, and even some adults, may be inclined to chew on the bedding.

Eliminate on Command

From the beginning it is important that you take your puppy out on leash to relieve himself. This will save you much time in the years to come. There will be times when you will want your dog to eliminate on command, such as when you're putting him to bed, leaving for the day, standing in the rain, taking him in the car or before entering the veterinarian's office. If the dog's needs are not taken care of, he may have an accident at an inappropriate time. There will be occasions when you will want your dog to relieve himself when he is on leash because being off leash could be dangerous. It is more difficult to teach this concept to the older dog who is not used to going on leash. The older dog is used to doing his own thing and is able to hold it for a longer period. Therefore, it is wise to teach the puppy while he is young.

If an accident happens and your puppy goes in the house, it works best to blot the spot with paper towels, then use a solution of water and white vinegar.

You will learn your puppy's defecation schedule. Puppies are always willing to urinate. If your pup was supposed to defecate on the walk outside and didn't, put him back in the crate and schedule another trip outside in about 30 minutes.

Many pet owners crate train and housetrain their Cockers and, when their dog is trustworthy, they eliminate the crate, giving the dog complete freedom of the house. If the crate is available, many dogs will continue to use it as their den. Other owners will crate their dogs only when they leave home. It's up to you, but the safest environment for your puppy is his crate or under your constant surveillance.

Other Equipment

Besides a crate, you will need some type of lead for exercising your puppy. You cannot leave a collar on the puppy in his crate, and it takes too long to fasten a buckle collar on a potty-anxious puppy. I like to use a slip lead (kennel-type noose). It works very well, since it is quick to put on and will tighten if the puppy fools around. You don't want to take a chance on your puppy getting loose and running off!

Like kids, puppies love to play.

You can also use a nylon web show lead or an obedience slip collar with the leash connected. You may want to look into the new adjustable nylon web collars that have a snap lock rather than a buckle. They are much easier to handle than the old-fashioned buckle collars. Usually these collars have matching nylon leads. The three-quarter-inch web collar and leash are satisfactory for the Cocker.

My personal preference is to use a metal or web choke collar and a four-foot leather leash. The leather leash is easier to grip during obedience training, and the choke collar prevents the dog from pulling out of a regular collar. A choke collar should not be left on an unsupervised dog! There is always the possibility the collar could get caught on something and choke your dog. The same goes for a collar with dog tags dangling from it; it is safer to have identification tags (rabies, dog license, i.d.) riveted onto the collar.

You may also want to purchase a pooper-scooper for your new puppy so you can scoop the yard daily. Keeping the yard clean is especially important if your puppy has worms. When the stool lays on the ground, there is a good chance your dog can be infected (see Chapter 7 for more on worms and other health concerns).

Fenced-in Yards

Fenced-in yards are a wonderful convenience, but they should never be trusted. Gates can accidentally be left open and some Cockers are notorious for digging under fences or scaling the tops. Fenced-in yards should never be used as a replacement for walking the puppy on a leash to teach housebreaking. Many dogs have been known to run around the yard, only to come back in the house to do their business. Leaving the dog outside for long periods of time does nothing to encourage housetraining, because the dog can relieve himself whenever he desires, and does not learn to hold it. Cockers are not meant to live their lives outside; they're happiest inside with their owners. Also, inclement weather is very hard on the Cocker's coat.

Puppy Proofing Your Home

Puppies will get into everything. I've heard of puppies being electrocuted from biting electrical cords, hanging themselves in the window-blind cords, ingesting objects that had to be surgically removed, drinking from toilets that contained cleaning chemicals, bloating themselves from raiding the garbage can or dog food bin, drowning from diving into the swimming pool—the list could go on forever.

HOUSEHOLD DANGERS

Curious puppies and inquisitive dogs get into trouble not because they are bad, but simply because they want to investigate the world around them. It's our job to protect our dogs from harmful substances, like the following:

IN THE HOUSE

cleaners, especially pine oil

perfumes, colognes, aftershaves

medications, vitamins

office and craft supplies

electric cords

chicken or turkey bones

chocolate

some house and garden plants, like ivy, oleander and poinsettia

IN THE GARAGE

antifreeze

garden supplies, like snail and slug bait, pesticides, fertilizers, mouse and rat poisons

You must learn to anticipate any trouble your puppy could get into. Make sure cabinet doors are securely closed, garbage is kept in a tightly-lidded container or behind a closed door, any medications are safely out of reach, potentially toxic plants are inaccessible, electric cords are secured to baseboards and small objects are stored away.

When you leave your puppy alone, make sure she has suitable chew toys and that she's confined in a room where she can't get into too much trouble. Otherwise, don't be surprised if the puppy goes for chair legs, the sofa or cabinets. Not only could your puppy harm herself by getting into any number of things, but she could kill herself with her destructive behavior—and it could be your fault. Animal shelters are full of dogs whose owners gave up on them because they were destructive. All puppies go through chewing everything and anything during teething, but unfortunately, some dogs never give up the habit.

Exercise

Exercise is important for the Cocker. Unfortunately, too many Cockers and other dogs are overweight. The proper exercise will help keep a dog's weight down and her heart and lungs functioning properly. If your dog is active and at her proper weight, she may be getting enough exercise on her own. Otherwise, it's your job to see that she gets exercise.

Happy dogs get plenty of exercise.

It's okay to let your dog run in the fenced-in yard a few minutes each day, but keep her under observation. Cockers do get bored and will look for ways to escape. Throwing a tennis ball for your dog several times a day provides great exercise.

In the Car with Your Cocker

It is not unusual for puppies to get carsick. The good news is that they usually outgrow it if they are exposed to travel on a regular basis. Until the puppy or adult is a seasoned traveler, it is best for the dog to travel on an empty stomach. Also, be sure she has had an opportunity to relieve herself.

Accidents do happen, so it's wise to carry a leash, paper towels, garbage bags, extra newspaper (for the crate) and terry cloth towels so you're prepared. I've found that some of my puppies do not outgrow this until they are about six to eight months of age. It is important that your puppy continues to travel; if the car sickness persists, your veterinarian can prescribe some medication that may help.

Your puppy should get used to going almost anywhere with you.

Most young puppies will ride better when they are allowed to sit on the seat or on someone's lap, although the safest place is in a fiberglass crate. If you are ever in a car accident and your dog's in her crate, you won't have to worry about her being thrown from the car or escaping through doors that are thrown open. Also, a crate is convenient if you need to leave your dog in the car while you run into the store. But *don't leave your dog for long!* She may be stolen or suffer from overheating in the car. If you'd rather not secure your dog in a crate, look into a safety harness.

Under no circumstances should you let your dog put her head out of an open window. Debris can be blown into her eyes. Also, never leave your dog unattended with a leash on. The dog could somehow strangle herself if the leash gets caught on something and she twists to break free.

Protecting Against Loss or Theft

Dog owners today have several options for identifying their dogs. There's the original dog tag, the tattoo and the microchip.

Keep your adorable puppy safe!

Although tags can be lost, they are the quickest and most easily recognized form of identification for your dog. You should make sure you have one on your dog's collar. You can also have your dog tattooed. It's a safe, easy, painless procedure. Your social security number or your dog's AKC registration number is tattooed on his inner thigh. Tattoos are permanent. To be effective, however, you must register the number (along with your name, address and phone number) with a tattoo registry organization. Your breeder, a local breed club or your veterinarian can help.

The microchip is another permanent method of identification. It's a rice-sized pellet that contains a computer chip inside a sheath of surgical glass. It's implanted by a simple injection between your dog's shoulder blades, where it causes no discomfort. The number encoded in the chip is registered along with your name, address and phone number.

The chip has to be "read" by a special scanner. Microchips are becoming more and more popular as a safe and permanent means of identification, but they have some disadvantages. Few people would think to look for a microchip, and if they did, they'd have to find a compatible scanner in order to have the chip read. Some veterinarians and animal shelters have them, but not all. Discuss your options with your veterinarian.

If you do lose your Cocker Spaniel, here are some tips for finding him. Whatever happens, don't give up:

- Check the local shelters every day. Calling may not be enough—you should make personal appearances. Some shelters only hold dogs for three days. There is always the possibility that your dog may not appear in a shelter for several days or weeks.

- Call your breeder. Breeders are sometimes contacted when a lost Cocker is found.

- Contact rescue groups. (See Chapter 13 for information on contacting rescue groups.)

- Advertise in the newspaper.

- Prepare flyers and post them at the local schools, grocery stores, gas stations, veterinary clinics, convenience stores and any other place that will allow them.

- Contact the local schools—children may have seen your dog.

- Advertise on the radio.

- Contact the road crews and sanitation departments—if your dog was hit by a car, they might have picked up the body.

chapter 5

Feeding
your
Cocker Spaniel

More than likely, the breeder will give you some food and instructions for your new puppy. This way, your puppy will not have to change his diet during those first few days, which are already stressful.

If, at a later time, either you or your veterinarian decides this is not the best diet, you can wean your puppy over to a new diet. Frequently, Cocker Spaniels are prone to digestive upsets when their diet is changed. Therefore, you should take five to seven days to wean him from one food to another.

Let's Talk Nutrition

Anything your dog eats and digests is a source of nutrition. What your dog actually gets out of what she eats depends on the food's digestability and how your dog's body uses the food. That's why there are good things to eat and bad things to eat.

There are six "building blocks" of nutrition: protein; carbohydrates; fat; vitamins; minerals; and water. Each is essential to the health of your dog. How do they work?

Protein Proteins are a varied group of biological compounds that affect many different bodily functions, including the immune system, cell structure and growth. Proteins are most commonly acquired from foods like meats, grains, dairy products and legumes. Being omnivores (meat and plant eaters) dogs can get protein from a number of sources. The body doesn't use all the protein it ingests, however, so more isn't necessarily better. What's more important is the quality of the protein. For dogs, meat is better than meat by-products or vegetables.

Carbohydrates Like proteins, carbohydrates serve many functions in the body, but their most important one is to supply energy. Carbohydrates help proteins do their job, too. Carbohydrates are acquired from bread, pasta, cereal, grains, potatoes, vegetables, rice and cookies—foods that contain starches, sugars and fiber. Excess carbohydrates are stored as fat for later use.

HOW MANY MEALS A DAY?

Individual dogs vary in how much they should eat to maintain a desired body weight—not too fat, but not too thin. Puppies need several meals a day, while older dogs may need only one. Determine how much food keeps your adult dog looking and feeling her best. Then decide how many meals you want to feed with that amount. Like us, most dogs love to eat, and offering two meals a day is more enjoyable for them. If you're worried about overfeeding, make sure you measure correctly and abstain from adding tidbits to the meals.

Whether you feed one or two meals, only leave your dog's food out for the amount of time it takes her to eat it—10 minutes, for example. Freefeeding (when food is available any time) and leisurely meals encourage picky eating. Don't worry if your dog doesn't finish all her dinner in the allotted time. She'll learn she should.

Fat Though the word has a negative connotation in our society, fats are very important for the body. They store energy, help absorb some vitamins, play a part in cell production and hormone function, and contribute to a healthy coat and skin. Best of all, they make food taste good. Unfortunately, too much fat leads to the problems that have given fat a bad name: obesity, heart disease and generally poor health.

Vitamins are vital elements necessary for growth and maintenance of life. There are water-soluble vitamins and fat-soluble vitamins. Water-soluble vitamins include the B and B-complex vitamins, C, thiamin, riboflavin, biotin and folic acid. Fat-soluble vitamins include A, D, E and K. Vitamin A contributes to vision, growth and skin texture. Carrots, fish oil and animal liver are excellent sources of Vitamin A. The B vitamins are necessary for normal cellular function; they're acquired through dairy products and meat. Vitamin C maintains the immune system and is derived from vegetables and citrus fruits.

Minerals Minerals (sometimes called "ash") are the fundamental building blocks of bone and teeth, and are also needed for cellular functions Minerals are obtained from food, water and salt. Some examples are iron, calcium, zinc, potassium and sodium.

Water Of all the nutrients, water is the most important. It's vital to all bodily functions, makes up about 70 percent of a dog's weight, and without it dehydration can occur within days.

Types of Food

There are four different types of commercial pet foods:

TYPES OF FOODS/TREATS

There are three types of commercially available dog food—dry, canned and semimoist—and a huge assortment of treats (lucky dogs!) to feed your dog. Which should you choose?

Dry and canned foods contain similar ingredients. The primary difference between them is their moisture content. The moisture is not just water. It's blood and broth, too, the very things that dogs adore. So while canned food is more palatable, dry food is more economical, convenient and effective in controlling tartar buildup. Most owners feed a 25% canned/75% dry diet to give their dogs the benefit of both. Just be sure your dog is getting the nutrition he needs (you and your veterinarian can determine this).

Semimoist foods have the flavor dogs love and the convenience owners want. However, they tend to contain excessive amounts of artificial colors and preservatives.

Dog treats come in every size, shape and flavor imaginable, from organic cookies shaped like postmen to beefy chew sticks. Dogs seem to love them all, so enjoy the variety. Just be sure not to overindulge your dog. Factor treats into her regular meal sizes.

1. generic

2. private label

3. those marketed in grocery and feed stores (popular brands)

4. those marketed in pet stores or veterinary clinics (premium brands)

The major differences between pet foods marketed nationally in grocery or feed stores (popular brands) and those sold exclusively in pet stores or veterinary clinics (premium brands) are: the variability and quality of ingredients used, and the emphasis on palatability versus nutrition.

Most popular pet foods are variable-formula diets. The ingredients used vary depending on their availability and cost. In contrast, many premium-brand pet foods are produced from fixed formulas, that is, the ingredients are not varied depending on cost.

I suggest you feed your Cocker Spaniel a fixed-formula diet. In the past I have used several variable-formula diets and have had problems with each one. As previously mentioned, Cockers can be prone to gastrointestinal upsets when their food is changed.

A snood (cloth tube) over your Cocker's head will keep his ears out of his food at mealtime.

I have found the variable-formula diets to be inconsistent, and the result in the puppy was always diarrhea. The fixed-formula diet is just that—fixed.

There are three forms of commercially-produced pet foods presently available: dry, semimoist and canned. Semimoist foods are high in sugar, are usually very palatable, have a long shelf life because of the high preservative content and produce large stool volume in the dog.

Canned foods are high in water—75 percent compared to 10 percent water in dry foods and 35 percent in semimoist foods. Canned foods are palatable, but are high in sodium nitrite, which acts as a diuretic in some dogs. Both canned and semimoist foods are expensive compared to dry food, and neither will enhance house-training. With these foods a larger volume of stool will be produced. Even more importantly, they will do nothing to help your dog's teeth.

Feeding your dog a premium dry food will decrease stool volume and produce firmer stools. Dry food aids in decreasing plaque buildup on the teeth—prevention of which promotes healthier gums and teeth.

Puppy Diet

Premium puppy-growth diets are formulated to meet the special needs of puppies. The puppy-growth diet should be fed to the Cocker Spaniel until she is about eight to twelve months old. Some of my eight- to nine-month-old puppies seem to become a bit bored with their food at that age. Then I know it is time to change to the adult-maintenance diet.

In the last few years some breeders have changed from the customary premium puppy-growth diets to lamb-based diets because more dogs are developing allergies. When this occurs, the dog needs to be put on a hypoallergenic diet. Generally the protein in these diets is derived from either lamb, venison, duck or

---

HOW TO READ THE DOG FOOD LABEL

With so many choices on the market, how can you be sure you are feeding the right food for your dog? The information is all there on the label—if you know what you're looking for.

Look for the nutritional claim right up top. Is the food "100% nutritionally complete"? If so, it's for nearly all life stages; "growth and maintenance," on the other hand, is for early development; puppy foods are marked as such, as are foods for senior dogs.

Ingredients are listed in descending order by weight. The first three or four ingredients will tell you the bulk of what the food contains. Look for the highest-quality ingredients, like meats and grains, to be among them.

The Guaranteed Analysis tells you what levels of protein, fat, fiber and moisture are in the food, in that order. While these numbers are meaningful, they won't tell you much about the quality of the food. Nutritional value is in the dry matter, not the moisture content.

In many ways, seeing is believing. If your dog has bright eyes, a shiny coat, a good appetite and a good energy level, chances are his diet's fine. Your dog's breeder and your veterinarian are good sources of advice if you're still confused.

---

rabbit—meats which elicit the least allergic response. I don't recommend switching to a hypoallergenic diet right away. It is best to feed using the customary diet consisting of beef until a problem arises. Otherwise, it may be difficult to find a diet with a protein to which the dog hasn't had previous exposure. Allergies generally develop through exposure. It is not unusual for a dog to eat the same diet for years and then develop an allergy to it.

Supplements

Some pet owners believe the misconception that "more is better." This can be quite harmful to your dog. Some commercial pet foods contain some nutrients in quantities that, if consumed over a prolonged period of time, may be harmful. Excessive nutrients can predispose or further the progression of diseases that affect the kidneys, heart, vascular system and skin. Urinary stones can also develop and the dog's growth can be stunted.

Your veterinarian is your best source for determining the proper diet for your Cocker Spaniel. But remember that a premium diet is a well-balanced one. Vitamins and other supplements can unbalance the balanced diet. Even adding canned food, unless it is the same brand and type (puppy dry and puppy canned by the same manufacturer) can throw off the balance.

Schedule

I recommend that you feed your puppy at the same times every day. I also suggest feeding him in his crate. He needs to eat undisturbed in a quiet place. If not, the puppy could be distracted and eat and run, eat and play, eat a little more and then quit. It is far better to give the puppy his food in the crate and give him 15 to 20 minutes to eat. After the time has elapsed, pick up the dish. If the puppy hasn't finished his food, refrain from offering him treats or other types of food. Give the puppy his next meal at the regular time. After a couple of days, you may realize you are feeding your puppy too much—adjust the portion appropriately. I like to feed my dogs in one-quart, stainless steel pans. A crockery bowl may work better for the young puppy. Your dog may use a plastic bowls as a chew toy.

The breeder will tell you how much to feed your new puppy. As your puppy grows you will need to increase the amount he is fed. Eventually, by the time he is about six to eight months old, the puppy could be eating approximately two cups of puppy food per day.

Your puppy should be fed three times a day until about four to six months of age. Generally, I feed equal portions at the morning and evening meals and a smaller portion at the noon meal. You can determine when to feed your puppy only two meals a day by observing if he starts to pick at his food. By six months of age, the puppy should be eating only twice a day. It is best to feed your puppy at the same times each day.

Do not give milk to your puppy. After he is about six weeks of age he no longer needs milk. Milk can cause diarrhea in puppies after that age, as well as in adults.

TO SUPPLEMENT OR NOT TO SUPPLEMENT?

If you're feeding your dog a diet that's correct for her developmental stage and she's alert, healthy-looking and neither over- nor underweight, you don't need to add supplements. These include table scraps as well as vitamins and minerals. In fact, a growing puppy is in danger of developing musculoskeletal disorders by over-supplementation. If you have any concerns about the nutritional quality of the food you're feeding, discuss them with your veterinarian.

Freefeeding and Meal Manners

I do not recommend that you "freefeed" your puppy or dog. That is, do not put the day's ration out for your dog to eat when she wants. If for no other reason than house-training, it is better for your puppy to eat at scheduled times. For behavioral reasons, much is to be gained by giving the puppy her food and then removing her dish, whether it is empty or not. You should teach your dog, as a puppy, that it is okay for you to pick up her food and then give it back. Some dogs are known to be very protective of their food; some may not tolerate children around their food dish. This is

another bonus of feeding in the crate—no one gets
hurt. Try to prevent problems, but teach your puppy
good manners, too.

Water

I am sure you realize the importance of clean, fresh
water for your puppy and dog. Water should be available to your dog at all times. The only exception is if
your young puppy is having a difficult time holding it
during the night. If this is the case, you can withhold
water from about 9 p.m. until early in the morning.
Usually if dogs have water available at all times, they
won't drink too heavily at one time, which can cause
vomiting. If you have a problem with this, you may
have to limit the amount until your puppy has learned
to drink in moderation.

I suggest you keep water in the crate so it is always
accessible. Because water bowls are easily tipped over,
hang a two-quart stainless steel water pail in the crate.
Except for the very small puppy, water pails work
best—there is less spillage, and your dog's ears will stay
dry while she is drinking.

Feeding the Adult Dog

Feed your adult dog a high-quality
maintenance diet. One way to
evaluate a food is by following a
manufacturer's dietary program
through the life stages—from
puppy to adult to senior. Ask your
breeder or veterinarian for a recommendation if you're not familiar with a particular food.

*Dogs need
different diets
at different
ages.*

Some owners prefer to feed their dogs twice a day
while others, myself included, feed only once a day.
There is the occasional dog that has trouble with just
one meal a day and who may vomit some bile-like fluid
in between meals. For such a dog, two meals a day is
preferable.

The average-sized adult Cocker eats approximately one and one-half to two cups of a premium food daily. Of course this varies with the individual dog and his lifestyle, whether he's active or spends most of his day napping.

Whatever amount works best for your Cocker, make sure you measure it out every day. That way, if your dog gets sick and the veterinarian wants to know how much he eats, you can give a specific answer. This will help the vet enormously. Food should be served at room temperature—never too hot or too cold.

Watching Your Dog's Weight

It is important that you keep an eye on your dog's weight. As most of us know, it doesn't take much to add an extra pound or two, and this could be serious for the Cocker Spaniel. A typical dog acts like she hasn't eaten for weeks. This is a sign of a normal, healthy dog. Usually, problems with obesity are related to the number of treats your dog has conned out of you.

Dogs do not need changes in their diets. If they are healthy and at normal weight, they don't get bored with their food. Avoid feeding table scraps. They don't fit into her balanced diet, will cause gastrointestinal upsets and can contribute to a weight problem. If you refrain from feeding your dog at the table, a begging habit shouldn't begin. If you like to feed treats, take them from your dog's daily ration of food. I suggest you measure her food, leave it on the kitchen counter or some other unreachable place, and hand out rewards from there.

Obesity is the most common nutritional disease in dogs. It can predispose your dog to heart, circulatory, liver, diabetic and pancreatic diseases. Your dog could experience heat intolerance and breathing difficulties. Cocker Spaniels are already predisposed to spinal problems; these can be exacerbated by obesity. Arthritis and torn ligaments are other problems overweight dogs suffer, simply by carrying too much weight around. Last but not least, anesthesia and surgery are a greater risk for obese dogs.

If your veterinarian recommends watching your dog's food intake, follow his or her advice. You can start by decreasing the food intake by one quarter. Canned carrots and green beans are acceptable fillers. One way of evaluating your dog's weight is by checking the amount of fat over her rib cage. You should be able to feel the dog's ribs easily. Your dog is overweight if you find it difficult to feel her ribs; she is obese if you can't feel them at all. If your dog is having a weight problem even on a reduced diet with plenty of exercise, ask your veterinarian to check her thyroid levels.

The Older Cocker's Diet

In my experience, the older Cocker Spaniel (nine to ten years old) will benefit from a diet of less protein and more fiber. I prefer keeping a little more weight on an older dog, but never to the point of obesity. Old dogs need some reserve weight for their inevitable decline. At this time of their lives, they won't gain weight as quickly as they can lose it. Discuss this with your veterinarian.

Several years ago I owned an eleven-year-old Cocker who showed signs of kidney problems. Her laboratory work did not confirm this. Nevertheless, I started her on a prescription diet (through my veterinarian) and she lived for another three years. Sometimes laboratory tests are a little behind the actual symptoms. Since then, I've started my older Cockers on diets with less protein. The old saying "You are what you eat" also applies to your pet.

chapter 6

Grooming
your
Cocker Spaniel

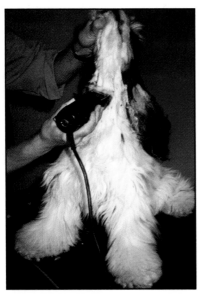

Grooming your Cocker can be a lot of fun, or just another chore. I like to think of it as a special time: a one-on-one situation (after all, we're best friends!) —our special time together. Grooming provides a wonderful opportunity to physically examine your dog (see Chapter 7 for more details on what you should be looking for). I want my dog to not only look the best he can, but also look like a Cocker Spaniel, not just a shaggy dog.

There are many reasons why you should keep your Cocker groomed on a regular schedule. The Cocker Spaniel is such an appealing and beautiful dog; most owners are proud to own one and want it to look its best at all times.

More importantly, some areas need to be trimmed short on a regular basis to prevent problems. The pertinent areas are the lip folds, around the eyes, the underside of the ears, and between the pads of the feet. If hair is allowed to grow in these areas, your dog can end up with a lip fold infection, conjunctivitis and mats between the toes, which can lead to sores because they're irritating and a dog will lick at them excessively. A dog with too much hair between its toes may even show signs of lameness. Long hair around the insides of the ears blocks off what little air is able to reach the ear canal. Keep it trimmed.

Give your Cocker a thorough grooming every 6–8 weeks—or take her to a professional.

Grooming Your Own Dog

Some pet owners prefer to have their Cocker professionally groomed. I would recommend a thorough grooming every six weeks—do not wait longer than eight weeks. Your dog will be much happier if you stick to this schedule.

When choosing a professional groomer it may be helpful to check out how well he or she gets along with Cockers. Some ill-tempered dogs don't appreciate having mats combed out; consequently, some groomers prefer not to bother with the breed. A groomer may not like Cockers, and if the dog senses the animosity, the problem will be compounded. Most dogs behave very well, and yours should, too, if you acquired him from an experienced breeder who exposed your puppy to regular trimmings at an early age.

The unkempt cocker is a groomer's challenge. This is especially true when the coat is matted and the owner wants to save it. When I am grooming pet owners' dogs, I explain that if there are any difficult mats I would prefer to cut them out. This is less stressful for the dog and, after all, the coat will grow back. Some owners prefer puppy cuts and others desire complete shave-downs. The puppy cut leaves longer hair, which is more attractive than the shaved-down dog.

EQUIPMENT

You can learn to groom your Cocker yourself. Two advantages of doing this are that you can groom your dog more frequently and you can also save money.

GROOMING
TOOLS

pin brush

slicker brush

flea comb

towel

matt rake

grooming
glove

scissors

nail clippers

tooth-
cleaning
equipment

shampoo

conditioner

clippers

If you intend to do any grooming at home, a grooming table is helpful, if not a requirement. Some people also use the grooming arm and noose, which are attached to the table. They, too, are helpful but not necessary. If you use the noose, do not leave your dog alone on the table. If he should jump, the noose could cause serious harm. Dogs can be easily table-trained not to jump.

The regular grooming table has a covering of non-slip matting over it. If a grooming table is out of your budget, then perhaps you can find some other type of table. I have known owners to use card tables, picnic tables or other small tables. Whatever type of table you use, it should be sturdy. If it wobbles, your dog will be frightened and uncooperative. Even if you plan to have your dog professionally groomed, a table comes in handy for the in-between combings.

To groom your Cocker, you need a first-class clipper. Before choosing one, inquire about service and which clipper blades are compatible with it. Eventually, you may want two or three different sizes of blades, but for now you should start with the #10, which is the most useful. I also like the #7F for trimming the back, the #40 for doing lip folds and the undersides of the ears, and the #15 for closer trimming of the face. I would suggest you buy them in this order, but you probably can do fine with just the #10 blade.

Besides clippers, you'll need a comb (I am partial to combs with one-inch teeth, nine teeth to an inch), a pin brush, a slicker brush, a pair of six- or seven-inch straight shears, a pair of single-sided thinning shears and a nail trimmer. In the beginning you can get by with a clipper, nail trimmer, comb and a pair of straight shears. Combs work better than brushes for taking out mats.

It is easiest to learn how to trim a Cocker if you are able to follow someone else's pattern. To do this, have your dog's breeder or groomer trim your Cocker, let his coat grow out for three or four weeks, then try it yourself. You will be able to see the hair that has grown out and identify what needs to be retrimmed. If you are afraid to try it, keep in mind all your mistakes will grow out and you can do better the next time.

Trim close to the opening of the ear.

The Trim

Few of us have the same method of starting a trim on a dog. I like to start trimming with a #10 blade on the ear, starting at the flap (which is about one-third of the way down), taking the clipper against the hair up to the top of the ear, and lifting the clipper a little when meeting the skull. The clipper is lifted so as not to dig into that area and create a ridge. Next I hold the ear up and clip the underside, trimming very close around the opening.

Pay particular attention to the lip fold areas and corners of the eyes.

At this point, I start trimming the muzzle and sides of the head, paying particular attention to the lip fold areas and the corners of the eyes. These areas need to be trimmed as close as possible. Trim the whiskers and

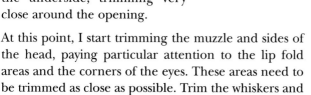

eyelashes. Long eyelashes are not proper on a sporting dog. Trim the top of the head with clippers and thinning scissors (or shears if thinning scissors are not available). Use the clippers, going *with* the hair, on the back half of the skull. The front half is thinned with thinning scissors, trying to give a domed appearance but not a "rooster" cut. This is impossible on some flat-skulled dogs.

I like to do the front of the neck next, taking the clipper against the hair. Some dogs are sensitive in this area. In my experience, I have not found this to be a problem unless the hair was allowed to grow too long. If that's the case, the clipper must be taken with the hair to get the length shorter, then against the hair to clean it up. Next, take the clipper, going with the hair, down the side of the neck, trying to blend it in. You would never use a clipper on the back of a show dog, but I routinely do this on pets. The #7 blade is better, leaving the coat a little longer than the #10. Clip carefully along the back, going with the hair, and a small way down the sides. You don't want to leave your dog with a "hula skirt." Of

Trim away hair under the feet, then shape the hair around them.

course, if your dog is severely matted, you may not have a choice. The dog's tail can be cleaned up with thinning scissors, shears or the clipper—don't leave feathers on it.

The legs can be a challenge. I like to clip the elbow and around it with a #10 blade. This area mats easily, so it's good to clip it to prevent mats from forming. You need to comb the legs as you're working. They can be scissored short (about two inches) for a puppy cut, or they can be left long. Cockers are currently being groomed so the hair is up on the legs and doesn't drape the floor. Start at the foot, shaping the hair on it with shears and trimming away hair under the feet so it's even with the foot. After the feet are done, you can layer the feathering on the legs, shortening the hair, starting at the foot. This isn't necessary, but if you feel creative you may want to give it a try.

Trimming the Nails

Don't be afraid to try to trim your dog's nails. Most dogs are quite tolerant of having their nails trimmed,

Before trimming...

but some misbehave. These dogs must be properly restrained so they don't get away with their antics. If they do, they'll continually struggle until they get their way. Ask your veterinarian or breeder how to handle your dog if he misbehaves.

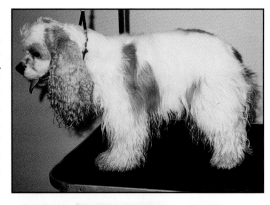

Unless your dog is black, you will probably find at least one light-colored nail on him. This will give you an idea where the blood supply stops. Your veterinarian or technician can show this to you. Nails that are not trimmed on a regular basis can end up tearing. This is painful and means a trip to the veterinarian

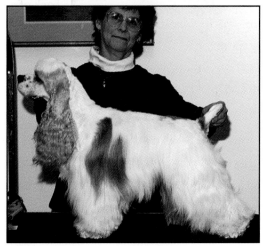

for a remedy. If you should cut a nail too close and cause it to bleed, sticking the nail in a soft piece of soap will stop the bleeding.

...and after. What a difference!

The Bath

Not all coat trimmings need to end with a bath; in-between trimmings are fine. I prefer to trim before bathing so I can trim any loose ends after the dog is dry. Before bathing it is important that you comb out any mats. If this is not done the dog will be harder to demat after drying.

I do believe in frequent baths, especially for puppies. They get dirty so quickly. The old way of thinking was that frequent baths were too drying to the skin. In my experience, this has not been a problem. Young puppies can be bathed as often as every seven to fourteen days, but it is imperative you do this in a warm, draft-free environment. You must also thoroughly dry the puppy with towels and a hair dryer. Your puppy will probably hate the hair dryer, but it is a necessary evil that he'll learn to tolerate.

In my opinion, frequent bathing helps prevent skin problems. It seems to keep down the growth of bacteria on the skin. Nevertheless, I have some older dogs living with "senior citizens" that have had very few baths in their lifetimes. They could surely stand a bath, but their skin is in excellent condition. Whether

Clip against the hair, starting about one-third down the ear.

bathing the puppy or the adult, it is important that the dog is kept warm and thoroughly dried. Damp skin can result in hot spots—raw patches of itchy skin.

The most important thing to remember about bathing is not to get water in the ears. You don't need to get the top of the head or the top of the ears wet. These areas are seldom dirty and can be sponged off satisfactorily. Water in the ears promotes ear infections. You also need to be careful when using soap around your dog's eyes. Rinse them well with cold water if you think soap could have splashed into the eyes.

A good grooming or conditioning shampoo purchased from your veterinarian or a pet shop will suffice to clean the average Cocker. There are many different types of shampoos available, especially for problem skins. Only your veterinarian should recommend a medicated shampoo. The different types control various problems, and you don't want to use them haphazardly—you could do damage to your dog's skin.

Last, but not least, you need to clean out the dog's ears with a drying agent and cotton balls. Squirt in a few drops of a solution made with equal amounts of 3 percent hydrogen peroxide and 70 percent alcohol, and wipe out the ears. This is very important after the bath, because you may have inadvertently gotten water into the ears.

There is nothing more pleasing to look at than a freshly groomed Cocker Spaniel. The dog looks truly loved.

chapter 7

Keeping your
Cocker Spaniel
Healthy

This chapter has four sections: maintenance (p. 64), the physical examination (p. 79), emergency care (p. 85) and geriatric care (p. 92). While all the information will help to keep your Cocker Spaniel healthy, it's especially important to be familiar with emergency care. Also, while helpful, this section is not a substitute for veterinary care. Don't hesitate to contact your veterinarian with any health concerns.

Maintenance

The Cocker Spaniel is generally a very hearty dog. With vaccinations and good health care, proper nutrition, regular grooming and enough exercise, you can expect your Cocker to live for twelve to fifteen years. I have known many to live even longer.

Your breeder probably recommended that you have your puppy or new dog checked by a veterinarian within 48 to 72 hours. The new puppy check up is customary and important because you want to be assured that your puppy is healthy. My personal recommendation to new pet owners is for them to wait about three days. This allows the puppy a chance to acclimate to her new owners and environment. Waiting a few days also gives the new owners an opportunity to observe the puppy and formulate questions for the veterinarian. All changes will be stressful for the young puppy. Nevertheless, it is important to have your puppy checked fairly early. You do not want to become attached to your puppy and then discover it has a serious problem.

VACCINATIONS

Vaccines are given to puppies starting at five or six weeks of age and continuing every two to three weeks until they're sixteen to twenty weeks old. I am referring to what is commonly known as the DHLPP, a vaccine for distemper, hepatitis, leptospirosis, parvovirus and parainfluenza. Depending upon where you live, the rabies vaccine is given at three or six months of age. Many breeders also vaccinate their puppies for tracheobronchitis, otherwise known as kennel cough. There is a vaccine for coronavirus, but it is not commonly given unless there is a problem in a community or kennel.

You may be wondering why it is necessary to give puppies so many vaccines. In order for a vaccine to give protection against disease, the puppy's maternal antibodies must be gone from the puppy. The maternal antibodies for distemper are gone sometime between

---

YOUR PUPPY'S VACCINES

Vaccines are given to prevent your dog from getting an infectious disease like canine distemper or rabies. Vaccines are the ultimate preventive medicine: they're given before your dog ever gets the disease so as to protect him from the disease. That's why it is necessary for your dog to be vaccinated routinely. Puppy vaccines start at eight weeks of age for the five-in-one DHLPP vaccine and are given every three to four weeks until the puppy is sixteen months old. Your veterinarian will put your puppy on a proper schedule and will remind you when to bring in your dog for shots.

eight and fourteen weeks of age. Maternal antibodies for parvovirus are usually gone by sixteen weeks of age. Much of this depends on the vaccination history of the dam and the environment in which she lived. You should not short-change your puppy. Even so, a thirteen to sixteen week old, well-vaccinated puppy may come down with parvo. This is usually a critical age

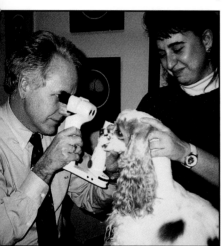

An eye exam is part of a thorough checkup.

because the maternal antibodies begin to diminish and the puppy can be infected through exposure.

Distemper is a virus that attacks every tissue in the body. It is carried by foxes, wolves, raccoons and mink, as well as dogs. Signs of distemper are similar to a bad cold with fever. It can cause pneumonia, runny eyes and nose, and diarrhea. With treatment, the dog may make a temporary recovery, which is followed by even more serious symptoms such as recurrent convulsions. Death is common. If the dog does recover, she may be disabled with nervous disorders. In my experience, this is not a curable disease. Unvaccinated youngsters and senior dogs are most susceptible.

Hepatitis is a virus spread by contact with an infected animal or its stool or urine. The disease affects the liver and kidneys and is characterized by high fever, depression and lack of appetite.

Leptospirosis is an infectious bacterial disease transmitted by contact with the urine of an infected dog, rat or other wildlife. It produces severe symptoms of fever, depression, jaundice and internal bleeding. The disease can be spread from dogs to humans.

Parvovirus is a virus that was first identified in the late 1970s. It attacks the intestinal tract and bone marrow. The heart muscle may also be affected in very young pups. Symptoms include depression, loss of appetite, vomiting, diarrhea and collapse.

Rabies is a viral disease spread through the saliva of infected animals, including raccoons, skunks, foxes, dogs and cats. It's transmitted through a bite. The disease attacks nerve tissues, resulting in paralysis and death. Rabies can be transmitted to people, and is virtually always fatal.

Tracheobronchitis *(kennel cough)* is caused by several organisms. Current vaccines are useful, but do not protect the dog against all strains. While tracheobronchitis is not life-threatening, it can progress to serious bronchopneumonia. Symptoms are coughing, sneezing, hacking and retching accompanied by nasal discharge lasting from a few days to several weeks. Dogs who routinely come in contact with other dogs at the groomer's boarding kennel or training class should be vaccinated regularly.

Coronavirus is another disease that typically occurs when many dogs are together, like in kennels. It's transmitted by contact with infected feces and urine, and causes depression, loss of appetite, vomiting that may contain blood, and moderate to severe diarrhea that's yellow-orange in color. It's not a life-threatening disease.

Lyme disease was first diagnosed in 1976 in the United States in Lyme, Connecticut. Lyme disease is carried by deer ticks and causes acute lameness, swelling of the joints and loss of appetite. If you notice any of these symptoms, have your dog tested for the disease. The sooner you begin treatment the better. A vaccine is available for Lyme disease; your veterinarian can tell you whether it's appropriate for your dog.

Three types of ticks (l-r): the wood tick, brown dog tick and deer tick.

After your puppy has received all of his shots, he should be revaccinated ("boostered") with DHLPP and parvo vaccines once a year. It is customary to booster rabies one year after the first vaccine and then, depending on where you live, every year or three years thereafter.

At the time of his annual veterinary visit, your Cocker should receive a thorough physical examination. If you've noticed any problems, write them down and take a list of questions with you. Don't forget to bring a fresh stool sample (just a small amount) so the vet can examine it for parasites. Depending on your veterinarian's policy, your visit could also include the annual heartworm test. Dogs must be checked before being put on heartworm preventive medication. Make sure your dog's weight is recorded. Also, make sure his ears are examined; some dogs have slight infections that can only be seen by the doctor's otoscope.

WHEN TO CALL THE VET

In any emergency situation, you should call your veterinarian immediately. You can make the difference in your dog's life by staying as calm as possible when you call and by giving the doctor or the assistant as much information as possible before you leave for the clinic. That way, the vet will be able to take immediate, specific action to remedy your dog's situation.

Emergencies include acute abdominal pain, suspected poisoning, snakebite, burns, frostbite, shock, dehydration, abnormal vomiting or bleeding, and deep wounds. You are the best judge of your dog's health, as you live with and observe him every day. Don't hesitate to call your veterinarian if you suspect trouble.

PARASITES

Internal parasites are an ever-present hazard for your dog. They are more prevalent in some areas than others, depending on the climate, soil and contamination. Your dog will certainly have a better chance of remaining worm-free if you routinely check for them (twice a year or more if there is a problem). Keep your dog in a fenced-in yard and pick up after him daily.

Eggs of parasites are passed in an animal's stool. They lie on the ground and become infective in a certain number of days depending on the type of worm. If your dog's stool sample tests positive for worms, you will be given a treatment for the dog and asked to bring back another sample in a certain number of days (depending on the type of worm). Rechecking and treatment should go on until the dog has at least two negative samples. The time between tests and treatments depends on the type of worm found in your dog. Different worms have different life cycles. *Do not buy over-the-counter wormers.* Different types of worms require different medications.

Ascarids or Roundworms are the most commonly found worms in both young and adult pets, and the most easily removed. The adult worms are round and whitish in color, generally three to four inches long or longer (spaghetti-like); they may be curled up. Frequently, they can be seen in the stool or may be vomited up by the dog. Roundworms may be passed to the puppy through the placenta or the mother's milk if she was infected. It is also possible to pick up this parasite through ingestion.

Common internal parasites (l-r): roundworms, whipworms, tapeworms and hookworms.

Hookworms are thin, threadlike and only half an inch long. They will look like white threads in the dog's stool, although it is difficult to see them. They are the most dangerous intestinal parasite. Hookworms attach to the lining of the intestine and literally pump blood from your pet. Like roundworms, hookworms can be passed to puppies from their mothers while they are in the womb, and through her milk. Hookworm eggs are passed in the stool, lie on the ground and become infective in a certain number of days. They're absorbed through the skin or ingested by the dog licking his contaminated feet.

Whipworms are not passed by the mother. The life cycle of a whipworm is three months, so they are not seen in puppies under three months of age. They are seldom noticed in the stool. Whipworms cause an intermittent diarrhea, usually with excess mucus. Whipworm eggs are resistant to most environmental factors, including freezing. In fact, they can survive in a frozen state for years until they are warmed enough to mature.

Tapeworms are one of the most common types of worms found in the pet, and possibly the most difficult to eliminate. They are long, flat and ribbonlike, sometimes several feet in length, and made up of many smaller segments. These small, ricelike segments can be seen around the pet's anus and at the base of the tail. Dogs most commonly become infected with tapeworms through contact with fleas, rabbits, rodents and certain large game, like deer. A tapeworm infestation is passed to your pet when he ingests adult fleas through licking and chewing, or if he eats an infected, dead mouse, deer or other wild animal.

Coccidium and giardiasis are two relatively common protozoal infections that usually affect young puppies, especially those housed in pet shops, kennels or other places where large numbers of puppies are brought together. Older animals usually do not show symptoms when infected unless they are under stress. Clinical signs of coccidiosis and giardiasis are diarrhea, weight loss and loss of appetite. These diseases are contracted by animals through licking their feet or licking contaminated food dishes in pens where the disease has existed.

These specks in your dog's fur mean he has fleas.

Heartworm disease is caused by an infection with a parasitic filarial roundworm that lives in the heart and adjacent blood vessels of the lung. A dog can be infected with one to several hundred adult heartworms, which grow from six to fourteen inches long. Heartworm is prevalent throughout the United States. Depending upon where you live, your dog should receive an annual or semiannual blood test. Heartworm disease is life-threatening, expensive to treat and *easily* prevented. Most veterinarians recommend that you keep your dog on year-round prevention, which may be given either once a month or daily.

External Parasites: Fleas, Ticks, Mange and Mites

Fleas are less expensive to prevent than to treat, but you have to be diligent to keep them at bay. Besides causing intense itching, many dogs are allergic to flea bites—so allergic that just one bite can cause the dog to lick, chew and bite himself raw, at which point medical attention is necessary.

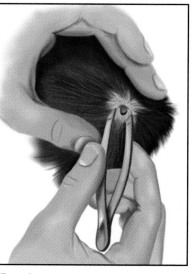

I have found that flea collars are not very effective on the Cocker-sized dog. Owners can buy flea-preventive pills, but these will not help a dog who's allergic to flea bites, because the medicine is not effective on fleas until after they bite the dog. There are sprays that kill adult fleas, their eggs and the larvae—I recommend that you use this type of spray if your dog is exposed to fleas. Most flea shampoos are not very effective.

Use tweezers to remove ticks from your dog.

I also recommend that you treat your home with a spray every few months. I prefer a long-lasting adulticide which contains the insect-growth regulator fenoxycarb. It is important to vacuum first, then spray the entire house, including upholstery, under the cushions and furniture, and around baseboards.

You should ask your veterinarian for advice on combining different products. If you are not careful, you could cause a toxic reaction in your dog. It is best to purchase your flea products from your veterinarian. Many of the over-the-counter products will not do the job for you.

The flea is a die-hard pest.

Ticks carry Rocky Mountain spotted fever, Lyme disease (discussed under Vaccines) and other diseases. Any ticks you see on your dog should be carefully

71

removed with tweezers; try not to pull the head out. Speak with your veterinarian about the best way to control ticks. Taking them off as soon as you see them is essential.

Sarcoptic Mange is caused by a mite. It is difficult to diagnose because it's hard to find the mite on skin scrapings. You'll know your dog has it if you notice itchy pimples with crusting and scaling along the edges of the ears, on the elbows and between the neck and chest. It causes intense itching, and is highly contagious to other dogs. Humans can get sarcoptic mites, but the mite is host-specific and will not live long on humans. This disease is easily treated by your veterinarian.

Demodectic Mange appears in youngsters aged three to ten months. It's passed to them by their mothers. It may start with small areas of hair loss around the eyes, lips or forelegs. There is little itching unless there is an accompanying bacterial infection. The disease is not contagious and is diagnosed by a skin scraping.

Cheyletiella is a small mite that lives in the outer layers of the skin. It causes intense itching and yellow-gray scales may be found on the dog's back, rump, top of the head and nose. The disease is diagnosed by a skin scraping.

FIGHTING FLEAS

Remember, the fleas you see on your dog are only part of the problem—the smallest part! To rid your dog and home of fleas, you need to treat your dog *and* your home. Here's how:

• Identify where your pet(s) sleep. These are "hot spots."

• Clean your pets' bedding regularly by vacuuming and washing.

• Spray "hot spots" with a non-toxic, long-lasting flea larvicide.

• Treat outdoor "hot spots" with insecticide.

• Kill eggs on pets with a product containing insect growth regulators (IGRs).

• Kill fleas on pets per your veterinarian's recommendation.

SPAYING AND NEUTERING

Spaying and neutering pets at an early age will prevent the occurrence of virtually all tumors of the reproductive tissues. Unspayed females are prone to mammary and ovarian cancer. During their later years, they may develop pyometra (an infection of the uterus), which is life threatening.

To prevent mammary tumors it is important to spay your female before her first heat cycle. Spaying consists of general surgery to remove the ovaries and uterus. It is considered major surgery, but Cockers handle it very well. Today's anesthetics make it possible for your dog to come home from the clinic a few hours after surgery.

Neutering the male at six months has much to offer besides the medical benefits. I have found that a male neutered at this age will not attain the habit of marking territory and hiking his leg indiscriminately. Intact males are susceptible to testicular cancer, perineal hernias, perianal fistulas, perianal tumors and prostatic disease. Surgery consists of removing both testicles and leaving the scrotum intact. It is a simple procedure, and your boy will walk out of the clinic a few hours after surgery.

Usually the intact male or female will need to be neutered or spayed at a later age because it will be the best way to treat a disease they've developed. Surgery is much harder on dogs if they are old. Both the intact male and female are likely to lapse in their house-training—the female will piddle frequently before, during and after her heat cycle, and the male is prone to marking territory (even in the house) if there is a female in heat nearby.

ADVANTAGES OF SPAY/NEUTER

The greatest advantage of spaying (for females) or neutering (for males) your dog is that you are guaranteed your dog will not produce puppies. There are too many puppies already available for too few homes. There are other advantages as well.

ADVANTAGES OF SPAYING

No messy heats.

No "suitors" howling at your windows or waiting in your yard.

Decreased incidences of pyometra (disease of the uterus) and breast cancer.

ADVANTAGES OF NEUTERING

Lessens male aggressive and territorial behaviors, but doesn't affect the dog's personality. Behaviors are often owner-induced, so neutering is not the only answer, but it is a good start.

Prevents the need to roam in search of bitches in season.

Decreased incidences of urogenital diseases.

Some owners initially reject the idea of spaying and neutering thinking their pet may gain weight after surgery. This is not true. I have had numerous Cockers spayed and neutered and none became overweight.

However, if your pet puts on an extra pound, which is probably due to some other reason, cut back on his food and exercise him more. Your dog will be healthier if she is spayed or he is neutered.

Check your dog's teeth frequently and brush them regularly.

ORAL CARE (TEETH AND GUMS)

Feeding a hard, dry kibble is helpful in keeping plaque build-up off the teeth. Another way you can help your Cocker is to brush her teeth two to three times a week, starting at a young age. Do not use human toothpaste, as it is irritating to the dog's stomach. Your veterinarian carries the proper toothpaste and toothbrush or finger brush.

Your dog's teeth probably will need to be cleaned professionally at least once a year, starting at two to four years of age. This is important. Infected teeth produce toxins and bacteria that are carried throughout the body via the blood. The bacteria contribute to various diseases, such as endocardditis (heart), hepatitis (liver), various joint diseases (septic arthritis) and kidney damage. Do not neglect this important procedure, and do try to practice at-home care. You will prolong your Cocker's life.

COMMON AILMENTS

Anal sacs *(glands)*. These are sacs associated with small scent glands on either side of the anus that may cause the dog discomfort when they are full. Anal sacs should empty when the dog has a bowel movement. Symptoms of impaction and inflammation are excessive licking under the tail and/or bloody or sticky discharge from the anal area. Your dog may also scoot along the floor trying to itch them. Increasing the fiber in the diet produces a firm stool that may help this problem. Many veterinarians do not recommend emptying the sacs unless there are symptoms present.

Most breeders, including myself, prefer to express the anal sacs on a regular basis during bathing. You express the sacs by pulling the tail straight up and squeezing the two sacs in and up toward the anus. A foul-smelling fluid will come out. Be careful, you could be squirted!

Atresia of the puncta *(closed tear ducts)*. Cocker Spaniels are prone to closed tear ducts, which may or may not need to be opened by a veterinarian. A closed tear duct may cause your dog to produce more tears, although many dogs with normal tear ducts are prone to tearing, as well. Have the ducts checked if your dog is tearing a lot. It is best to wait until the dog is about six months old.

Cherry eye *(hypertrophy of nictitans glands)*. This is a common ailment in Cockers, as well as other short-nosed breeds. You may notice a red, cherry-like gland showing in the corner of the eye. This is not a medical emergency, but you should take the dog to the veterinarian as soon as possible. Frequently, the gland can be pushed back to its normal place and, treated with an ophthalmic, antibiotic, steroid ointment, it may regress. Cherry eye is usually a bilateral problem that occurs in puppies during stressful periods, such as teething. Even if the cherry eye regresses, it may re-appear days, weeks or months later. Veterinarians used to remove cherry eyes surgically, but today's recommendation is to tack them in place. Surgical removal does tend to lead to dry eye later in the dog's life.

Colitis is intermittent inflammation of the colon. Some Cocker bloodlines are more susceptible to this than others. The stool may be bloody or blood-tinged. Colitis could be the result of undiagnosed whipworms or stress. Sometimes it happens for no explainable reason. Frequently the dog feels fine and is willing to eat. At-home treatment could consist of Pepto Bismol, withholding food for 24 hours and then reintroducing small amounts of food with more fiber. If the condition persists or the dog is acting poorly, you should seek professional help.

Conjunctivitis is common in Cockers. The conjunctiva is the pink tissue that lines the inner surface of the eyelids and covers the front portions of the eyeball, except the clear, transparent cornea. The conjunctiva may become reddened, swollen and damaged by irritating substances such as bacteria, foreign matter or chemicals. It is important to keep the hair trimmed close around the eyes. Long hair stays damp and contributes to the problem. Try cleaning the dog's eyes with warm water and wipe away any matter that has accumulated in the corner of the eyes. If this doesn't keep conjunctivitis under control, you should see your veterinarian. Allergies may be the culprit.

Dry eye (*keratoconjunctivitis sica*) is a disease in which tear production is absent or decreased. The cornea dries out and becomes painful, and can result in loss of vision. It is a common problem in Cockers and may be immune-mediated or the result of cherry-eye removal. There may be other causes. Sometimes a white-gray discharge can be found around the eye, which may be yellow in color if the condition has persisted for awhile. If you do see this, have your dog's tear production checked. I have found tear production can vary, so you may need to check it more than once. Fortunately,

A FIRST-AID KIT

Keep a canine first-aid kit on hand for general care and emergencies. Check it periodically to make sure liquids haven't spilled or dried up, and replace medications and materials after they're used. Your kit should include:

Activated charcoal tablets

Adhesive tape
(1 and 2 inches wide)

Antibacterial ointment
(for skin and eyes)

Aspirin (buffered or enteric coated, *not* Ibuprofen)

Bandages: Gauze rolls (1 and 2 inches wide) and dressing pads

Cotton balls

Diarrhea medicine

Dosing syringe

Hydrogen peroxide (3%)

Petroleum jelly

Rectal thermometer

Rubber gloves

Rubbing alcohol

Scissors

Tourniquet

Towel

Tweezers

a drug is available 2 percent Cyclosporin) that effectively keeps this condition under control.

Ear infection *(otitis externa)*. This is an inflammation of the external ear canal that begins at the outside opening of the ear and extends inward to the eardrum. Cocker Spaniels are well known for their ear problems, which many people attribute to their long, pendulous ears (which certainly don't help). A dog's allergies—food and inhalant—along with hypothyroidism and other hormonal imbalances, contribute significantly to chronic ear infections. Uninformed owners mistakenly think that their pets are scratching their ears because of ear mites. In actuality, ear mites are not common in the adult dog. Allergies, however, are!

What can you do? Prevention of ear infections is most important. It is best that a dog never gets water in her ears. Water provides a good medium for bacteria to grow. If water should get in the ears, it is best to add a drying agent. Your veterinarian can provide such a product. Many of these medications can also be used routinely to clean the ears. An at-home preparation consisting of equal parts of 3 percent hydrogen peroxide and 70 percent rubbing alcohol, or equal parts of white vinegar and water can be used. Cotton-tip applicators can be used, but you must be careful to clean only what you see. It is possible, to damage the ear drum or pack debris down into the canal.

Cockers need regular ear care because of their pendulous ears.

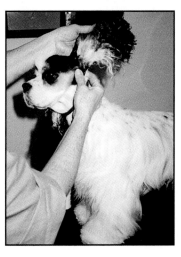

The ears will frequently require more aggressive cleaning if an infection is present. Your veterinarian may recommend sedating your dog and flushing the ears with either a bulb syringe or a Water Pik. The process may need to be done several times until the infection is under control. There is little value in treating dirty ears, because the medication will not come into contact with the ear canal. Your veterinarian may recommend that you bring the dog back at least every two weeks until the infection is gone. If the infection recurs in the near future or becomes chronic, the veterinarian may suggest further testing and/or a hypoallergenic diet on a trial basis (usually ten to twelve weeks). The veterinarian may also recommend a dermatologist for your dog.

If ears are not properly cared for, they may get so infected that surgery may be required at some time. Have your veterinarian explain proper ear maintenance before there is a problem.

Ear margin seborrhea The ear margins may have small, greasy plugs adhering to the skin. This is common in some dogs with pendulous ears, and may be a permanent problem. You can remove the accumulated material with your thumbnail and wash the areas with dandruff shampoo twice a week (ask your vet which shampoo to use). I have found using a snood on the dog during feeding decreases the problem (a snood is a cloth wrap that acts like a headband to keep a dog's ears from falling into its food or water).

Healthy Cockers are the favorites of the very young . . . and very old.

Flea bite allergy is caused by hypersensitivity (allergy) to flea saliva. The bite of one flea can cause the dog to bite, lick and scratch itself raw. Depending on the amount of discomfort and inflammation, your dog may need medical attention. You should immediately treat your dog and its environment for fleas. Trim and wash the involved area on your dog, daily if it is oozing any discharge, and treat with an antibiotic, anti-inflammatory product. These inflamed areas are commonly called hot spots.

Interdigital cysts are very common in Cockers. They are small swellings between the toes, usually associated with a staphylococcus (bacterial) infection. A home remedy is to soak the affected foot in a couple of quarts of water two times a day for two to three days. Make sure you dry the foot after the soak. If the cysts become a recurring problem, surgery may be required.

Lameness may be caused by something as simple as an interdigital cyst or mat between the toes, so this is the first area to check. Try to determine which leg is affected. If your dog is not putting weight on his leg, then he needs to be seen by the veterinarian. Otherwise, you may want to observe the dog for a couple of days. Try to remember if he has fallen, jumped or done something to hurt himself.

Lip fold pyoderma is a nuisance problem. Dogs who hypersalivate are at the greatest risk. The best prevention is to keep the hair cut short along the lip folds. Depending on the dog, trimming may need to be done on a weekly basis. Wash the area with an iodine scrub once a day, or more frequently depending on the severity. Chronic infections may require surgical resection of the lip fold.

Tonsillitis Dogs with tonsillitis may have a fever, eat poorly, swallow with difficulty and retch up white, frothy mucus. Tonsillitis is very contagious, and usually occurs in young dogs. Older dogs normally develop resistance to the disease. Medical treatment generally cures the condition. Rarely do the tonsils need to be removed.

The Physical Examination

Every pet owner should recognize what is normal for their dog and do periodic check-ups at home (approximately every month), so as to be promptly aware if something appears abnormal. You, the owner, will be the first to notice a change in your dog's appearance

Living with a
Cocker
Spaniel

or behavior. You should always pay attention to your dog's eating and elimination habits, as well as the way he moves. Being able to take your dog's temperature and check his gums and heart rate are important steps toward making sure your dog's as healthy as possible. *With careful observation and routine physicals, you will enhance the care of your dog and aid your veterinarian in diagnosing illness.*

IDENTIFYING YOUR DOG

It's a terrible thing to think about, but your dog could somehow, someday, get lost or stolen. How would you get him back? Your best bet would be to have some form of identification on your dog. You can choose from a collar and tags, a tattoo, a microchip or a combination of these three.

Every dog should wear a buckle collar with identification tags. They are the quickest and easiest way for a stranger to identify your dog. It's best to inscribe the tags with your name and phone number; you don't need to include your dog's name.

There are two ways to permanently identify your dog. The first is a tattoo, placed on the inside of your dog's thigh. The tattoo should be your social security number or your dog's AKC registration number.

The second is a microchip, a rice-sized pellet that's inserted under the dog's skin at the base of the neck, between the shoulder blades. When a scanner is passed over the dog, it will beep, notifying the person that the dog has a chip. The scanner will then show a code, identifying the dog. Microchips are becoming more and more popular and are certainly the wave of the future.

TAKING YOUR DOG'S TEMPERATURE

A dog's normal temperature is 100.5 to 102.5 degrees Fahrenheit. Use a rectal thermometer. With your dog standing, shake down the thermometer, then lubricate the end with some petroleum jelly. Insert the thermometer approximately one inch (less on a young puppy) and hold on to it while you're waiting so it isn't sucked into or expelled from the anus. Keep the thermometer inside the dog for one minute. If your dog's excited, his temperature may be higher than normal, so it would be wise to check it again later.

CHECKING GUM COLOR

Correct gum color is very important. Check it periodically when your dog is in good health so you can recognize anything abnormal—a sure sign that your dog is not feeling well. There may be black pigmentation around the gums, but in general, they should be bright pink, like yours. There should never be any yellowish tint to the gums. Pale gums suggest shock or anemia and are definitely signs of an emergency.

If you suspect a problem, press your thumb against the gum, which will whiten the spot. When you remove your thumb, time how long it takes for the spot to turn pink again. Normal capillary refill time (the time it takes for the pink color to return) is one to two seconds.

Heart Rate and Pulse

The heart rate in healthy Cockers is usually around 100 to 120 beats per minute. You can determine the heartbeat by placing your fingers against the dog's chest just below her elbow. Count the number of beats in a minute.

Measure your dog's pulse by placing your fingers on her femoral artery, located in the groin area. Find the artery by feeling along the inner thigh where the leg and body meet. A normal pulse rate should be the same as the heartbeat.

The heartbeat in a healthy dog depends on her size and condition. It is faster in small dogs and puppies and slower in large dogs or those in good physical condition.

Eyes

Cockers have beautiful eyes; therefore, it should be easy to notice anything out of the ordinary in them. Check the cornea (the clear part of the eye). Is it bright and shiny? Are the pupils of equal size? Do they constrict in response to light? Are the pupils black, or is there a gray-blue haziness or white cloudiness in them? Many old dogs have a blue haziness in their pupils, which may be

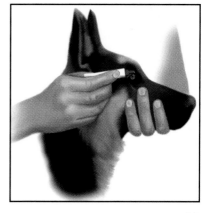

Squeeze eye ointment into the lower lid.

a normal aging change, though you should confirm any changes with your veterinarian.

Is the third eyelid (nictitans) partially protruding over the eye? Is there discharge or evidence of tearing? Is the white of the eye (sclera) reddened or discolored? The white of the eye should never appear yellowish. Are the pink mucous membranes that surround the eye (conjunctiva) pale, normal or irritated? A conjunctivitis or dry, dull-looking cornea could be the result of dry eye, which needs professional care. In my opinion, a prolapsed third eyelid, abnormal pupil size, cloudiness of the cornea or redness to the upper scleral area all constitute a visit to the veterinarian as soon as possible.

EARS

Every Cocker owner should routinely check their dog's ears—every week for normal dogs, more frequently if there's a problem. Do the ears have an odor? Are

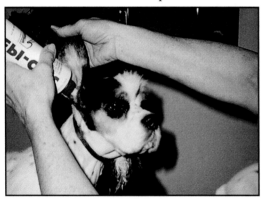

they clean or filled with gunk? If there's gunk in them, is it wet, dry, dark, creamy or bloody? Check for swelling. Your dog can have swollen, reddened ears but no infection; regardless, this condition needs to be checked by your veterinarian. Is your

Applying ear ointment.

dog shaking her head or scratching her ears a lot? Are the ears painful to the dog? Can your dog hear? Some older dogs lose their hearing. Unfortunately, there is no cure for deafness.

MOUTH

Check your dog's mouth and get him used to your handling of it. Is there brown or yellow build-up (calculus) around the teeth? Calculus can cause the gums to recede, which results in premature loosening of the teeth (periodontal disease). Inflammation and redness around the gum (gingivitis) is usually secondary to the presence of calculus. Are there any tumors inside or outside the mouth? Check the lip folds for infection.

SKIN AND COAT

Is the coat shiny or dry and brittle? Are there areas of thinning hair or hair loss (alopecia)? Does your dog have an itching problem (pruritis)? Can you see skin lesions or red, inflamed areas (erythema)? How about fleas and ticks: Does your dog have any of those? Is there an abnormal odor to the skin; any irritations or swellings between the toes? These are all conditions to look for and, if detected, to treat as soon as possible with veterinary assistance.

NOSE

A healthy dog's nose is usually cool and moist. However, the temperature or wetness of the dog's nose is not necessarily an indication of the dog's health. A sick dog may have a warm, dry nose, or a cool wet one. Look for other signs if you suspect a health problem.

Run your hands regularly over your dog to feel for any injuries.

Any secretion from the nose should be clear and watery, not thick, cloudy or colored. Most dogs have noses that are black, brown or liver-colored. There are Cockers that may have pink spots on their noses. These may or may not fill in as the dog ages. Redness or irritation could be indicative of an injury or sensitivity to sunlight. Some senior dogs have dry-looking noses.

BREATHING

Is your dog coughing or sneezing? Feel along his throat: Does touching it there cause the dog to cough more? Is his breathing shallow or deep? Anything abnormal should be reported to your veterinarian.

URINARY AND REPRODUCTIVE SYSTEMS

Is your dog drinking and urinating frequently? Does he or she urinate a normal amount or small amounts more frequently? Does he or she strain while urinating? Is there blood present?

Check your female for any vaginal discharge. Has she been licking herself? Vaginitis is quite common in female puppies before their first heat cycle. Check your female's mammary glands (breasts and nipples). Examine each one carefully for any bumps; report anything unusual to your veterinarian immediately.

Examination of the male's reproductive system starts at the penis. A small amount of thick, greenish discharge may be present in normal adult males, but is not usually present in neutered males. This discharge should be washed off and treated if it persists. Excessive licking or irritation of the prepuce (front of the penile shaft) results in redness or pain upon examination. If your dog is not neutered, examine his scrotum. Is the skin irritated, thickened or discolored? Palpate each testicle. Are they symmetric and uniform in size and shape? Is there any pain on examination of the scrotum or testes? Again, report anything unusual immediately.

NERVOUS SYSTEM

Is your dog bright and alert or is there evidence of mental depression, listlessness and lethargy? Is the dog walking and trotting normally, or does he appear off or lame? Does your Cocker have a stumbling or uncoordinated gait? Is he unwilling to jump into the car or go up and down stairs? Is there any sign of facial paralysis? Early signs are a drooping lip and eye, sometimes with salivation, and a slow blink on the affected side. Later signs are an atrophied lip and ear. The ear could be drawn up and carried a little higher.

Injury to the brain may manifest itself as a head tilt, though that could also be a sign of middle-ear infection. A brain injury can also cause nystagmus, an involuntary rapid horizontal or vertical movement of the eyeballs. Aimless wandering in circles or pressing the head against the wall or other objects indicates brain injury. Pain, weakness or paralysis of the forelegs or hind legs may indicate spinal cord damage. Sometimes the back is arched or the neck appears stiff. Emergency care is of the utmost importance.

 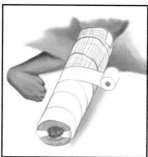

Make a temporary splint by wrapping the leg in firm casing, then bandaging it.

Emergency Care

Make it a point to familiarize yourself with your veterinarian: Keep his or her phone number by the telephone; know his or her policy for after-hours care; find out where the emergency clinic is and go there when it's not an emergency so you'll be prepared when one arises. *If you have a real emergency, time is of the essence.* The more familiar you are with all aspects of emergency care, the better chance you'll have of possibly saving your dog's life.

WHAT CONSTITUTES AN EMERGENCY?

As previously mentioned, pale gums and an abnormal heart rate could indicate that your dog is in shock, which constitutes an emergency (see the sections on temperature and heart rate under "The Physical Examination"). A very lethargic dog or one in shock needs treatment as soon as possible. Any dog hit by a car or suffering from a similar kind of trauma needs to be checked by the veterinarian. Even if your dog appears to be okay he should have chest and abdominal X rays taken to rule out serious injury.

Spinal paralysis needs to be treated as soon as possible—this condition needs medical treatment within a few hours of onset. Spinal problems need to be handled very carefully, with dogs kept confined and quiet until they get to the vet.

The rest of the conditions discussed range from mild to serious emergencies. Read about them now so you'll have a better idea of how to handle them if they happen to your dog.

ANTIFREEZE POISONING

Antifreeze is a potential killer. Dogs like it because it is sweet, and they'll be attracted to any spills in your garage or driveway. The prognosis for antifreeze poisoning is poor. A test is now available to confirm antifreeze ingestion; if you suspect it in your dog, have him tested immediately.

An Elizabethan collar keeps your dog from licking a fresh wound.

BEE STINGS

Bee stings can constitute an emergency if your dog is stung a lot or has an allergic reaction to them. Symptoms are swelling around the muzzle and face. Check the gum color immediately. Monitor swelling, keep checking gum color and pay attention to your dog's breathing. A severe reaction can cause difficulty in breathing, collapse and, sometimes, death.

BLEEDING

Apply a clean bandage to a wound tightly enough to prevent blood from dripping through, but not so tightly as to stop the circulation. Gauze is better than cotton, because cotton will stick to the wound. A small towel or clean wash cloth could serve as a bandage, secured with a stocking, scarf or necktie, if a regular bandage is not immediately available. Anything more serious than a scrape or small cut (both of which should be washed and dressed with antibiotic ointment) requires a visit to the veterinarian.

BURNS

Rinse a burn with cool water right away. Burns cause pain and even shock if enough of the area is exposed. Call your veterinarian immediately; burns can be very debilitating. With proper care, the skin should slough off in about three weeks; if the burn is severe, hair loss could be permanent.

CARDIOPULMONARY RESUSCITATION (CPR)

To perform CPR on your dog, lay him on his right side. Place your hands on either side of the dog's chest. Press firmly and release 70 times per minute. Pull the tongue forward to stimulate breathing. Alternately, for every six chest compressions, breathe once into the dog's nose—inhale, completely cover the dog's nose with your mouth, and exhale gently; don't blow hard. You should see the chest expand. Repeat every five to six seconds. Continue pressing on the chest. Call your veterinarian for further instructions, and make sure you keep your dog warm.

CHOCOLATE TOXICOSIS

Ten ounces of milk chocolate (a large candy bar) can kill a 12-pound dog. Chocolate toxicosis is a common problem because dogs like chocolate. Caffeine and theobromine, two basic chemicals in chocolate, over-stimulate a dog's nervous system. Symptoms of chocolate toxicosis may include restlessness, vomiting, increased heart rate, seizure or coma. Death is possible. If you know your Cocker has eaten chocolate, give her some syrup of Ipecac at a dosage of one-eighth teaspoon per pound.

CHOKING

If you notice that your dog is choking, open her mouth wide to see if any object is visible. Try to remove the object. Extend her neck and pull her tongue forward to help remove anything. If you don't see anything but she's still choking, lay her on her side and apply abdominal thrusts by sqeezing sharply just below the ribs. Call your veterinarian immediately.

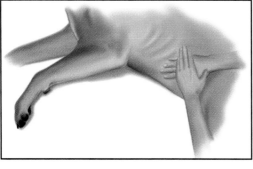

Applying abdominal thrusts can save a choking dog.

DOG BITES

If you are bitten by your dog or any other dog, wash the area immediately with soap and water. Find out when the dog had a rabies shot and when you were last vaccinated for tetanus. Call your doctor for information.

If your dog bites someone and she does not have a current rabies vaccine, she needs to be confined and observed for ten days, during which time she cannot receive a vaccination.

If your dog is bitten by another dog or animal, wash the area thoroughly. Whether you take your dog to the vet depends on the severity and location of the wound. Your dog may need to have the wound professionally cleaned and stitched. Again, you need to know the rabies status of your dog and the offending animal, if possible.

DROWNING

Remove any debris your dog may have swallowed and hold it upside down, swinging him gently a few times. Pull the tongue forward to stimulate breathing. Apply CPR, and call your veterinarian. If the dog has been exposed to very cold water, wrap him in blankets.

ELECTROCUTION

If you see your dog being electrocuted by chewing on an electric cord, for example, *turn off the current before touching him.* Try to resuscitate your dog by performing CPR and pulling the tongue forward to stimulate breathing. If your dog isn't breathing, try mouth-to-muzzle resuscitation. Don't give up, and call the vet pronto.

EYES

In Cocker Spaniels, any redness to the upper white part of the eye constitutes an emergency. Redness indicates inflammation. If something is in your dog's eye, rinse it thoroughly with cold water.

FISHHOOKS

Don't try to pull the hook out of your dog; go to your veterinarian. The hook needs to be cut off at the shank and pushed through. This probably needs to be done under sedation.

FOREIGN OBJECTS

It is amazing what dogs will swallow. I've assisted in numerous surgeries in which all kinds of objects have been removed from a dog's stomach or intestinal tract—even a corn cob!

Keep hydrogen peroxide on hand. If you see your dog eat something like a sock, you may be lucky enough to get him to vomit the object if you administer the peroxide within the hour. Give two tablespoons for the adult Cocker and call your veterinarian. Try to keep your dog from swallowing objects by keeping them out of his reach or away from it altogether. If your dog does swallow something, watch his bowel movements for a couple of days to see if the object passes through; surgery is expensive and occasionally not successful, especially if performed too late.

HEATSTROKE

Classic signs of heatstroke are rapid, shallow breathing, rapid heartbeat, a temperature above 104 degrees Fahrenheit and subsequent collapse. It's important to cool your dog off as quickly as possible. Spray or sponge him down with cool water and pack ice around the head, neck and groin. Monitor the dog's temperature and stop the cooling process when it reaches 103 degrees; continue to monitor the temperature to be sure it doesn't go back up. In any case, get veterinary attention immediately.

MUZZLE

Dogs who are in pain may try to bite you out of fear. You need to be able to restrain the dog so that this doesn't happen. The easiest way is to tie his mouth with something like a two-foot bandage or a piece of cloth, like a necktie or stocking, or piece of rope. Make a large loop by tying a loose knot in the middle of the cloth. Hold the ends up, one in each hand. Slip the loop over the dog's muzzle and lower jaw, just behind its nose. Quickly tighten the loop so the dog can't open his mouth. Next, tie the ends under the lower jaw. Make a knot there and bring the ends back on each side of the dog's face, under the ears. Tie the ends

Use a scarf or old hose to make a temporary muzzle, as shown.

together behind the ears at the back of the head. If you have never tried to do anything like this, you may want to give it a practice try when you are calm and it's not an emergency. If your dog tries to vomit, take the muzzle off right away to prevent him from breathing the vomit into his lungs and choking.

POISONING

Symptoms of poisoning include muscle trembling and weakness, increased salivation, vomiting and loss of bowel control. A dog can be poisoned by numerous things, including toxins in garbage. Various poisons are treated differently, so it's not always wise to induce vomiting.

Call your veterinarian immediately if you suspect poisoning. Knowing the source will help your vet immensely. Keep the numbers of a local poison control center (if you have one) and the national poison control center by the phone.

Some of the many household substances harmful to your dog.

PORCUPINE QUILLS

These can be very painful. They have barbs on the end of them that dig into the skin. They should not be pulled out; rather, they need to be pushed through. It's best to have your veterinarian remove them under sedation.

SEIZURE (CONVULSION OR FIT)

Generally, a seizure is not considered an emergency unless it lasts longer than 10 minutes. However, you should notify your veterinarian the next day if it occurs during the night. Cockers (as well as other breeds) may be predisposed to seizures. Dogs do not swallow their tongues; however, handling the mouth should be avoided, because you may be accidentally bitten. Loss of consciousness, defecating or urinating may or may not occur. Keep your dog in a safe place so he doesn't fall off furniture, down the stairs or bang his head into anything.

SHOCK

Shock is life-threatening and demands immediate veterinary care. It can occur after injury or even after severe fright. Other causes are hemorrhage, fluid loss, poisoning or collapse of a body system.

Symptoms of shock are a rapid, weak pulse; shallow breathing; dilated pupils; subnormal temperature and muscle weakness. Gum color is slow to return. Keep your dog warm while taking him to the vet.

SKUNK SPRAY

Being sprayed by a skunk is not really a life-threatening emergency, but it would be in my house! The old remedy is to wash the dog in tomato juice, followed by a soap and water bath. You can also try bathing the dog in a mixture that consists of one quart three-percent hydrogen peroxide, one-quarter cup baking soda and one teaspoon liquid soap, or you can try one of the new deskunking formulas available at pet supply stores.

Geriatric Care

There will come a time when you realize your Cocker Spaniel is a "senior citizen." The dog may be nine or ten years old, perhaps younger or older; he may be having a little trouble getting up, moving a little slower and sleeping more. The coat on some older dogs becomes quite gray, though this can start on very young dogs if they have a certain gene, and it's not always an indication.

Many geriatric dogs become arthritic and need to be handled gently. After I developed arthritis I understood why some arthritic dogs are inclined to bite! Your veterinarian can prescribe the proper medication to help relieve the pain.

Deafness is a problem that can result from chronic ear problems or advanced age. Deaf dogs respond well to hand signals, especially if they've learned them earlier in life. You need to be aware of the deaf dog's whereabouts at all times. If he wanders off, he's not going to respond to your calling of his name. Also, be careful not to sneak up on the deaf dog; he can't hear you and could be startled.

The older dog's eyesight may diminish, or he may go completely blind. Blind dogs adjust amazingly well to their familiar environment. If your senior citizen is experiencing vision problems, he should be checked out by an ophthalmologist to ensure that he is not in pain, or that he doesn't need treatment.

Regular veterinary care and diet adjustments are important for the geriatric dog. Your veterinarian may recommend a geriatric profile starting at age nine or ten. This profile could include a complete blood count, a chemical profile, a urinalysis, a thyroid test, a chest X ray and an electrocardiogram. Hopefully no organ dysfunction will be found, but if it is, treatment can be started. This should be done every six months to a year.

To give a pill, open the mouth wide, then drop it in the back of the throat

This is not the time to forego dental treatment! Anesthetics are safer than ever and, consequently, less stressful to the dog.

Some older dogs have periods of incontinence. Your veterinarian can prescribe medication that will help control this problem, but you need to give your older dog more opportunities to relieve himself.

It's best not to keep an older dog at a boarding kennel. Perhaps you can make arrangements for him to be taken care of in his own environment, or perhaps a veterinary technician can care for him.

Some people may consider introducing a younger dog into the household. Years ago, I owned an ailing ten-year-old and purchased two puppies. Those puppies actually rejuvenated my old gal, and she lived another few years. However, you must be careful; most senior citizens wouldn't take too kindly to a rambunctious youngster. Whatever you do, make sure you pay more attention to your older dog than the newcomer.

SAYING GOOD-BYE

There will be a time when you have to make one of the hardest decisions in your life: when to end your dog's life. As much as we would prefer it, aging dogs don't usually die quietly in their sleep. In most cases, it is kinder to elect euthanasia. Dogs seem to realize when they aren't the healthy dogs they used to be; they appear sorry when they have accidents. I don't think we should rob them of what little dignity they have left when their health goes. As loving pet owners, we need to spare our pets when possible. *Quality of life is what counts.* Remember the good times and say good-bye.

Your Happy, Healthy Pet

Your Dog's Name _____

Name on Your Dog's Pedigree (if your dog has one) _____

_____

Where Your Dog Came From _____

_____

Your Dog's Birthday _____

Your Dog's Veterinarian

    Name _____

    Address _____

    Phone Number_____

    Emergency Number_____

Your Dog's Health

    Vaccines

    type _____ date given _____

    type _____ date given _____

    type _____ date given _____

    type _____ date given _____

    Heartworm

    date tested _____ type used_____ start date _____

Your Dog's License Number_____

Groomer's Name and Number _____

Dogsitter/Walker's Name and Number_____

Awards Your Dog Has Won

    Award _____ date earned _____

    Award _____ date earned _____

Enjoying

your

Dog

chapter 8

Basic
Training

by Ian Dunbar, Ph.D., MRCVS

Training is the jewel in the crown—the most important aspect of doggy husbandry. There is no more important variable influencing dog behavior and temperament than the dog's education: A well-trained, well-behaved and good-natured puppydog is always a joy to live with, but an untrained and uncivilized dog can be a perpetual nightmare. Moreover, deny the dog an education and she will not have the opportunity to fulfill her own canine potential; neither will she have the ability to communicate effectively with her human companions.

Luckily, modern psychological training methods are easy, efficient, effective and, above all, considerably dog-friendly and user-friendly.

Doggy education is as simple as it is enjoyable. But before you can have a good time play-training with your new dog, you have to learn what to do and how to do it. There is no bigger variable influencing the success of dog training than the *owner's* experience and expertise. *Before you embark on the dog's education, you must first educate yourself.*

Basic Training for Owners

Ideally, basic owner training should begin well *before* you select your dog. Find out all you can about your chosen breed first, then master rudimentary training and handling skills. If you already have your puppy-dog, owner training is a dire emergency—the clock is ticking! Especially for puppies, the first few weeks at home are the most important and influential days in the dog's life. Indeed, the cause of most adolescent and adult problems may be traced back to the initial days the pup explores her new home. This is the time to establish the *status quo*—to teach the puppydog how you would like her to behave and so prevent otherwise quite predictable problems.

In addition to consulting breeders and breed books such as this one (which understandably have a positive breed bias), seek out as many pet owners with your breed as you can find. Good points are obvious. What you want to find out are the breed-specific *problems,* so you can nip them in the bud. In particular, you should talk to owners with *adolescent* dogs and make a list of all anticipated problems. Most important, *test drive* at least half a dozen adolescent and adult dogs of your breed yourself. An 8-week-old puppy is deceptively easy to handle, but she will acquire adult size, speed and strength in just four months, so you should learn now what to prepare for.

Puppy and pet dog training classes offer a convenient venue to locate pet owners and observe dogs in action. For a list of suitable trainers in your area, contact the Association of Pet Dog Trainers (see chapter 13). You may also begin your basic owner training by observing other owners in class. Watch as many classes and test drive as many dogs as possible. Select an upbeat, dog-friendly, people-friendly, fun-and-games, puppydog pet training class to learn the ropes. Also, watch training videos and read training books. You must find out what to do and how to do it *before* you have to do it.

Principles of Training

Most people think training comprises teaching the dog to do things such as sit, speak and roll over, but even a 4-week-old pup knows how to do these things already. Instead, the first step in training involves teaching the dog human words for each dog behavior and activity and for each aspect of the dog's environment. That way you, the owner, can more easily participate in the dog's domestic education by directing her to perform specific actions appropriately, that is, at the right time, in the right place and so on. Training opens communication channels, enabling an educated dog to at least understand her owner's requests.

In addition to teaching a dog *what* we want her to do, it is also necessary to teach her *why* she should do what we ask. Indeed, 95 percent of training revolves around motivating the dog *to want to do* what we want. Dogs often understand what their owners want; they just don't see the point of doing it—especially when the owner's repetitively boring and seemingly senseless instructions are totally at odds with much more pressing and exciting doggy distractions. It is not so much the dog that is being stubborn or dominant; rather, it is the owner who has failed to acknowledge the dog's needs and feelings and to approach training from the dog's point of view.

The Meaning of Instructions

The secret to successful training is learning how to use training lures to predict or prompt specific behaviors—to coax the dog to do what you want *when* you want. Any highly valued object (such as a treat or toy) may be used as a lure, which the dog will follow with her eyes and nose. Moving the lure in specific ways entices the dog to move her nose, head and entire body in specific ways. In fact, by learning the art of manipulating various lures, it is possible to teach the dog to assume virtually any body position and perform any action. Once you have control over the expression of the dog's behaviors and can elicit any body position or behavior at will, you can easily teach the dog to perform on request.

Teach your dog words for each activity she needs to know, like down.

Tell your dog what you want her to do, use a lure to entice her to respond correctly, then profusely praise and maybe reward her once she performs the desired action. For example, verbally request "Tina, sit!" while you move a squeaky toy upwards and backwards over the dog's muzzle (lure-movement and hand signal), smile knowingly as she looks up (to follow the lure) and sits down (as a result of canine anatomical engineering), then praise her to distraction ("Gooood Tina!"). Squeak the toy, offer a training treat and give your dog and yourself a pat on the back.

Being able to elicit desired responses over and over enables the owner to reward the dog over and over. Consequently, the dog begins to think training is fun. For example, the more the dog is rewarded for sitting, the more she enjoys sitting. Eventually the dog comes to realize that, whereas most sitting is appreciated, sitting immediately upon request usually prompts especially enthusiastic praise and a slew of high-level rewards. The dog begins to sit on cue much of the time, showing that she is starting to grasp the meaning of the owner's verbal request and hand signal.

WHY COMPLY?

Most dogs enjoy initial lure-reward training and are only too happy to comply with their owners' wishes. Unfortunately, repetitive drilling without appreciative feedback tends to diminish the dog's enthusiasm until she eventually fails to see the point of complying anymore. Moreover, as the dog approaches adolescence she becomes more easily distracted as she develops other interests. Lengthy sessions with repetitive exercises tend to bore and demotivate both parties. If it's not fun, the owner doesn't do it and neither does the dog.

Integrate training into your dog's life: The greater number of training sessions each day and the *shorter* they are, the more willingly compliant your dog will

become. Make sure to have a short (just a few seconds) training interlude before every enjoyable canine activity. For example, ask your dog to sit to greet people, to sit before you throw her Frisbee and to sit for her supper. Really, sitting is no different from a canine "Please."

To train your dog, you need gentle hands, a loving heart and a good attitude.

Also, include numerous short training interludes during every enjoyable canine pastime, for example, when playing with the dog or when she is running in the park. In this fashion, doggy distractions may be effectively converted into rewards for training. Just as all games have rules, fun becomes training . . . and training becomes fun.

Eventually, rewards actually become unnecessary to continue motivating your dog. If trained with consideration and kindness, performing the desired behaviors will become self-rewarding and, in a sense, your dog will motivate herself. Just as it is not necessary to reward a human companion during an enjoyable walk in the park, or following a game of tennis, it is hardly necessary to reward our best friend—the dog— for walking by our side or while playing fetch. Human company during enjoyable activities is reward enough for most dogs.

Even though your dog has become self-motivating, it's still good to praise and pet her a lot and offer rewards once in a while, especially for a good job well done. And if for no other reason, praising and rewarding others is good for the human heart.

PUNISHMENT

Without a doubt, lure-reward training is by far the best way to teach: Entice your dog to do what you want and then reward her for doing so. Unfortunately, a human shortcoming is to take the good for granted and to moan and groan at the bad. Specifically, the dog's many good behaviors are ignored while the owner focuses on punishing the dog for making mistakes. In extreme cases, instruction is *limited* to punishing mistakes made by a trainee dog, child, employee or husband, even though it has been proven punishment training is notoriously inefficient and ineffective and is decidedly unfriendly and combative. It teaches the dog that training is a drag, almost as quickly as it teaches the dog to dislike her trainer. Why treat our best friends like our worst enemies?

Punishment training is also much more laborious and time consuming. Whereas it takes only a finite amount of time to teach a dog what to chew, for example, it takes much, much longer to punish the dog for each and every mistake. Remember, *there is only one right way!* So why not teach that right way from the outset?!

To make matters worse, punishment training causes severe lapses in the dog's reliability. Since it is obviously impossible to punish the dog each and every time she misbehaves, the dog quickly learns to distinguish between those times when she must comply (so as to avoid impending punishment) and those times when she need not comply, because punishment is impossible. Such times include when the dog is off leash and 6 feet away, when the owner is otherwise engaged (talking to a friend, watching television, taking a shower, tending to the baby or chatting on the telephone) or when the dog is left at home alone.

Instances of misbehavior will be numerous when the owner is away, because even when the dog complied in the owner's looming presence, she did so unwillingly. The dog was forced to act against her will, rather than molding her will to want to please. Hence, when the owner is absent, not only does the dog know she need not comply, she simply does not want to. Again, the trainee is not a stubborn vindictive beast, but rather the trainer has failed to teach. Punishment training invariably creates unpredictable Jekyll and Hyde behavior.

Trainer's Tools

Many training books extol the virtues of a vast array of training paraphernalia and electronic and metallic gizmos, most of which are designed for canine restraint, correction and punishment, rather than for actual facilitation of doggy education. In reality, most effective training tools are not found in stores; they come from within ourselves. In addition to a willing dog, all you really need is a functional human brain, gentle hands, a loving heart and a good attitude.

In terms of equipment, all dogs do require a quality buckle collar to sport dog tags and to attach the leash (for safety and to comply with local leash laws). Hollow chew toys (like Kongs or sterilized longbones) and a dog bed or collapsible crate are musts for housetraining. Three additional tools are required:

1. specific lures (training treats and toys) to predict and prompt specific desired behaviors;

2. rewards (praise, affection, training treats and toys) to reinforce for the dog what a lot of fun it all is; and

3. knowledge—how to convert the dog's favorite activities and games (potential distractions to training) into "life-rewards," which may be employed to facilitate training.

The most powerful of these is *knowledge*. Education is the key! Watch training classes, participate in training classes, watch videos, read books, enjoy play-training with your dog and then your dog will say "Please," and your dog will say "Thank you!"

Housetraining

If dogs were left to their own devices, certainly they would chew, dig and bark for entertainment and then no doubt highlight a few areas of their living space with sprinkles of urine, in much the same way we decorate by hanging pictures. Consequently, when we ask a dog to live with us, we must teach her *where* she may dig, *where* she may perform her toilet duties, *what* she may chew and *when* she may bark. After all, when left at home alone for many hours, we cannot expect the dog to amuse herself by completing crosswords or watching the soaps on TV!

Also, it would be decidedly unfair to keep the house rules a secret from the dog, and then get angry and punish the poor critter for inevitably transgressing rules she did not even know existed. Remember: Without adequate education and guidance, the dog will be forced to establish her own rules—doggy rules—and most probably will be at odds with the owner's view of domestic living.

Since most problems develop during the first few days the dog is at home, prospective dog owners must be certain they are quite clear about the principles of housetraining *before* they get a dog. Early misbehaviors quickly become established as the *status quo*—

becoming firmly entrenched as hard-to-break bad habits, which set the precedent for years to come. Make sure to teach your dog good habits right from the start. Good habits are just as hard to break as bad ones!

Ideally, when a new dog comes home, try to arrange for someone to be present as much as possible during the first few days (for adult dogs) or weeks for puppies. With only a little forethought, it is surprisingly easy to find a puppy sitter, such as a retired person, who would be willing to eat from your refrigerator and watch your television while keeping an eye on the newcomer to encourage the dog to play with chew toys and to ensure she goes outside on a regular basis.

POTTY TRAINING

To teach the dog where to relieve herself:

1. never let her make a single mistake;
2. let her know where you want her to go; and
3. handsomely reward her for doing so:
    "GOOOOOOOD DOG!!!" liver treat, liver treat, liver treat!

Preventing Mistakes

A single mistake is a training disaster, since it heralds many more in future weeks. And each time the dog soils the house, this further reinforces the dog's unfortunate preference for an indoor, carpeted toilet. *Do not let an unhousetrained dog have full run of the house.*

When you are away from home, or cannot pay full attention, confine the dog to an area where elimination is appropriate, such as an outdoor run or, better still, a small, comfortable indoor kennel with access to an outdoor run. When confined in this manner, most dogs will naturally housetrain themselves.

If that's not possible, confine the dog to an area, such as a utility room, kitchen, basement or garage, where elimination may not be desired in the long run but as an interim measure it is certainly preferable to doing it all around the house. Use newspaper to cover the floor of the dog's day room. The newspaper may be used to soak up the urine and to wrap up and dispose of the feces. Once your dog develops a preferred spot for eliminating, it is only necessary to cover that part of the floor with newspaper. The smaller papered area may then be moved (only a little each day) towards the door to the outside. Thus the dog will develop the tendency to go to the door when she needs to relieve herself.

Never confine an unhousetrained dog to a crate for long periods. Doing so would force the dog to soil the crate and ruin its usefulness as an aid for housetraining (see the following discussion).

Teaching Where

In order to teach your dog where you would like her to do her business, you have to be there to direct the proceedings—an obvious, yet often neglected, fact of life. In order to be there to teach the dog *where* to go, you need to know *when* she needs to go. Indeed, the success of housetraining depends on the owner's ability to predict these times. Certainly, a regular feeding schedule will facilitate prediction somewhat, but there is nothing like "loading the deck" and influencing the timing of the outcome yourself!

Whenever you are at home, make sure the dog is under constant supervision and/or confined to a small

The first few weeks at home are the most important and influential in your dog's life.

area. If already well trained, simply instruct the dog to lie down in her bed or basket. Alternatively, confine the dog to a crate (doggy den) or tie-down (a short, 18-inch lead that can be clipped to an eye hook in the baseboard near her bed). Short-term close confinement strongly inhibits urination and defecation, since the dog does not want to soil her sleeping area. Thus, when you release the puppydog each hour, she will definitely need to urinate immediately and defecate every third or fourth hour. Keep the dog confined to her doggy den and take her to her intended toilet area each hour, every hour and on the hour.

When taking your dog outside, instruct her to sit quietly before opening the door—she will soon learn to sit by the door when she needs to go out!

Teaching Why

Being able to predict when the dog needs to go enables the owner to be on the spot to praise and reward the dog. Each hour, hurry the dog to the intended toilet area in the yard, issue the appropriate instruction ("Go pee!" or "Go poop!"), then give the dog three to four minutes to produce. Praise and offer a couple of training treats when successful. The treats are important because many people fail to praise their dogs with feeling . . . and housetraining is hardly the time for understatement. So either loosen up and enthusiastically praise that dog: "Wuzzzer-wuzzer-wuzzer, hoooser good wuffer den? Hoooo went pee for Daddy?" Or say "Good dog!" as best you can and offer the treats for effect.

Following elimination is an ideal time for a spot of play-training in the yard or house. Also, an empty dog may be allowed greater freedom around the house for the next half hour or so, just as long as you keep an eye out to make sure she does not get into other kinds of mischief. If you are preoccupied and cannot pay full attention, confine the dog to her doggy den once more to enjoy a peaceful snooze or to play with her many chew toys.

If your dog does not eliminate within the allotted time outside—no biggie! Back to her doggy den, and then try again after another hour.

As I own large dogs, I always feel more relaxed walking an empty dog, knowing that I will not need to finish our stroll weighted down with bags of feces!

Beware of falling into the trap of walking the dog to get her to eliminate. The good ol' dog walk is such an enormous highlight in the dog's life that it represents the single biggest potential reward in domestic dogdom. However, when in a hurry, or during inclement weather, many owners abruptly terminate the walk the moment the dog has done her business. This, in effect, severely punishes the dog for doing the right thing, in the right place at the right time. Consequently, many dogs become strongly inhibited from eliminating outdoors because they know it will signal an abrupt end to an otherwise thoroughly enjoyable walk.

Instead, instruct the dog to relieve herself in the yard prior to going for a walk. If you follow the above instructions, most dogs soon learn to eliminate on cue. As soon as the dog eliminates, praise (and offer a treat or two)—"Good dog! Let's go walkies!" Use the walk as a reward for eliminating in the yard. If the dog does not go, put her back in her doggy den and think about a walk later on. You will find with a "No feces—no walk" policy, your dog will become one of the fastest defecators in the business.

If you do not have a backyard, instruct the dog to eliminate right outside your front door prior to the walk. Not only will this facilitate clean up and disposal of the feces in your own trash can but, also, the walk may again be used as a colossal reward.

CHEWING AND BARKING

Short-term close confinement also teaches the dog that occasional quiet moments are a reality of domestic living. Your puppydog is extremely impressionable during her first few weeks at home. Regular confinement at this time soon exerts a calming influence over the dog's personality. Remember, once the dog is housetrained and calmer, there will be a whole lifetime ahead for the dog to enjoy full run of the house and garden. On the other hand, by letting the newcomer have unrestricted access to the entire household and allowing her to run willy-nilly, she will most certainly develop a bunch of behavior problems in short order, no doubt necessitating confinement later in life. It would not be fair to remedially restrain and confine a dog you have trained, through neglect, to run free.

When confining the dog, make sure she always has an impressive array of suitable chew toys. Kongs and sterilized longbones (both readily available from pet stores) make the best chew toys, since they are hollow and may be stuffed with treats to heighten the dog's interest. For example, by stuffing the little hole at the top of a Kong with a small piece of freeze-dried liver, the dog will not want to leave it alone.

Remember, treats do not have to be junk food and they certainly should not represent extra calories. Rather, treats should be part of each dog's regular

daily diet: Some food may be served in the dog's bowl for breakfast and dinner, some food may be used as training treats, and some food may be used for stuffing chew toys. I regularly stuff my dogs' many Kongs with different shaped biscuits and kibble.

Make sure your puppy has suitable chew toys.

The kibble seems to fall out fairly easily, as do the oval-shaped biscuits, thus rewarding the dog instantaneously for checking out the chew toys. The bone-shaped biscuits fall out after a while, rewarding the dog for worrying at the chew toy. But the triangular biscuits never come out. They remain inside the Kong as lures, maintaining the dog's fascination with her chew toy. To further focus the dog's interest, I always make sure to flavor the triangular biscuits by rubbing them with a little cheese or freeze-dried liver.

To teach come, call your dog, open your arms as a welcoming signal, wave a toy or a treat and praise for every step in your direction.

If stuffed chew toys are reserved especially for times the dog is confined, the puppydog will soon learn to enjoy quiet moments in her doggy den and she will quickly develop a chew-toy habit— a good habit! This is a simple *autoshaping* process; all the owner has to do is set up the situation and the dog all but trains herself— easy and effective. Even when the dog is given run of the house, her first inclination will be to indulge her rewarding chew-toy habit rather than destroy less-attractive household articles, such as curtains, carpets, chairs and compact disks. Similarly, a chew-toy chewer will be less inclined to scratch and chew herself excessively. Also, if the dog busies herself as a recreational chewer, she will be less inclined to develop into a recreational barker or digger when left at home alone.

Stuff a number of chew toys whenever the dog is left confined and remove the extra-special-tasting treats when you return. Your dog will now amuse herself with her chew toys before falling asleep and then resume playing with her chew toys when she expects you to return. Since most owner-absent misbehavior happens right after you leave and right before your expected return, your puppydog will now be conveniently preoccupied with her chew toys at these times.

Come and Sit

Most puppies will happily approach virtually anyone, whether called or not; that is, until they collide with adolescence and

develop other more important doggy interests, such
as sniffing a multiplicity of exquisite odors on the
grass. Your mission, Mr./Ms. Owner, is to teach and
reward the pup for coming reliably, willingly and
happily when called—and you have just three months
to get it done. Unless adequately reinforced, your puppy's tendency to approach people will self-destruct by
adolescence.

Call your dog ("Tina, come!"), open your arms (and
maybe squat down) as a welcoming signal, waggle a
treat or toy as a lure and reward the puppydog when
she comes running. Do not wait to praise the dog until she reaches you—she may come 95 percent of the
way and then run off after some distraction. Instead,
praise the dog's *first* step towards you and continue
praising enthusiastically for *every* step she takes in your
direction.

When the rapidly approaching puppy dog is three
lengths away from impact, instruct her to sit ("Tina,
sit!") and hold the lure in front of you in an outstretched hand to prevent her from hitting you mid-
chest and knocking you flat on your back! As Tina
decelerates to nose the lure, move the treat upwards
and backwards just over her muzzle with an upwards
motion of your extended arm (palm-upwards). As the
dog looks up to follow the lure, she will sit down (if she
jumps up, you are holding the lure too high). Praise
the dog for sitting. Move backwards and call her again.
Repeat this many times over, always praising when Tina
comes and sits; on occasion, reward her.

For the first couple of trials, use a training treat both as
a lure to entice the dog to come and sit and as a reward
for doing so. Thereafter, try to use different items as
lures and rewards. For example, lure the dog with a
Kong or Frisbee but reward her with a food treat. Or
lure the dog with a food treat but pat her and throw a
tennis ball as a reward. After just a few repetitions, dis-
pense with the lures and rewards; the dog will begin to
respond willingly to your verbal requests and hand signals just for the prospect of praise from your heart and
affection from your hands.

Instruct every family member, friend and visitor how to get the dog to come and sit. Invite people over for a series of pooch parties; do not keep the pup a secret—let other people enjoy this puppy, and let the pup enjoy other people. Puppydog parties are not only fun, they easily attract a lot of people to help *you* train *your* dog. Unless you teach your dog how to meet people, that is, to sit for greetings, no doubt the dog will resort to jumping up. Then you and the visitors will get annoyed, and the dog will be punished. This is not fair. *Send out those invitations for puppy parties and teach your dog to be mannerly and socially acceptable.*

Even though your dog quickly masters obedient recalls in the house, her reliability may falter when playing in the backyard or local park. Ironically, it is *the owner* who has unintentionally trained the dog *not* to respond in these instances. By allowing the dog to play and run around and otherwise have a good time, but then to call the dog to put her on leash to take her home, the dog quickly learns playing is fun but training is a drag. Thus, playing in the park becomes a severe distraction, which works against training. Bad news!

Instead, whether playing with the dog off leash or on leash, request her to come at frequent intervals—say, every minute or so. On most occasions, praise and pet the dog for a few seconds while she is sitting, then tell her to go play again. For especially fast recalls, offer a couple of training treats and take the time to praise and pet the dog enthusiastically before releasing her. The dog will learn that coming when called is not necessarily the end of the play session, and neither is it the end of the world; rather, it signals an enjoyable, quality time-out with the owner before resuming play once more. In fact, playing in the park now becomes a very effective life-reward, which works to facilitate training by reinforcing each obedient and timely recall. Good news!

Sit, Down, Stand and Rollover

Teaching the dog a variety of body positions is easy for owner and dog, impressive for spectators and extremely useful for all. Using lure-reward techniques, it is possible to train several positions at once to verbal commands or hand signals (which impress the socks off onlookers).

Sit and *down*—the two control commands—prevent or resolve nearly a hundred behavior problems. For example, if the dog happily and obediently sits or lies down when requested, she cannot jump on visitors, dash out the front door, run around and chase her tail, pester other dogs, harass cats or annoy family, friends or strangers. Additionally, "Sit" or "Down" are the best emergency commands for off-leash control.

It is easier to teach and maintain a reliable sit than maintain a reliable recall. *Sit* is the purest and simplest of commands—either the dog is sitting or she is not. If there is any change of circumstances or potential danger in the park, for example, simply instruct the dog to sit. If she sits, you have a number of options: Allow the dog to resume playing when she is safe, walk up and put the dog on leash or call the dog. The dog will be much more likely to come when called if she has already acknowledged her compliance by sitting. If the dog does not sit in the park—train her to!

Stand and *rollover-stay* are the two positions for examining the dog. Your veterinarian will love you to distraction if you take a little time to teach the dog to stand still and roll over and play possum. Also, your vet bills will be smaller because it will take the veterinarian less time to examine your dog. The rollover-stay is an especially useful command and is really just a variation of the down-stay: Whereas the dog lies prone in the traditional down, she lies supine in the rollover-stay.

As with teaching come and sit, the training techniques to teach the dog to assume all other body positions on cue are user-friendly and dog-friendly. Simply give the appropriate request, lure the dog into the desired body position using a training treat or toy and then *praise* (and maybe reward) the dog as soon as she complies. Try not to touch the dog to get her to respond. If you teach the dog by guiding her into position, the dog will quickly learn that rump-pressure means sit, for example, but as yet you still have no control over your dog if she is just 6 feet away. It will still be necessary to teach the dog to sit on request. So do not make training a time-consuming two-step process; instead, teach the dog to sit to a verbal request or hand signal from the outset. Once the dog sits willingly when requested, by all means use your hands to pet the dog when she does so.

To teach *down* when the dog is already sitting, say "Tina, down!," hold the lure in one hand (palm down) and lower that hand to the floor between the dog's forepaws. As the dog lowers her head to follow the lure, slowly move the lure away from the dog just a fraction (in front of her paws). The dog will lie down as she stretches her nose forward to follow the lure. Praise the dog when she does so. If the dog stands up, you pulled the lure away too far and too quickly.

When teaching the dog to lie down from the standing position, say "Down" and lower the lure to the floor as before. Once the dog has lowered her forequarters and assumed a play bow, gently and slowly move the lure *towards* the dog between her forelegs. Praise the dog as soon as her rear end plops down.

After just a couple of trials it will be possible to alternate sits and downs and have the dog energetically perform doggy push-ups. Praise the dog a lot, and after half a dozen or so push-ups reward the dog with a training treat or toy. You will notice the more energetically you move your arm—upwards (palm up) to get the dog to sit, and downwards (palm down) to get the dog to lie down—the more energetically the dog responds to your requests. Now try training the dog in silence and you will notice she has also learned to respond to hand signals. Yeah! Not too shabby for the first session.

To teach *stand* from the sitting position, say "Tina, stand," slowly move the lure half a dog-length away from the dog's nose, keeping it at nose level, and praise the dog as she stands to follow the lure. As soon

Using a food lure to teach sit, down and stand. 1) "Phoenix, sit." 2) Hand palm upwards, mov lure up and back over dog's muzzle. 3) "Good sit, Phoenix!" 4) "Phoenix, down." 5) Hand palm down wards, move lure down to lie between dog's forepaws. 6) "Phoenix, off. Good down, Phoenix! 7) "Phoenix, sit!" 8) Palm upwards, move lure up and back, keeping it close to dog's muzzle. 9) "Goo sit, Phoenix!"

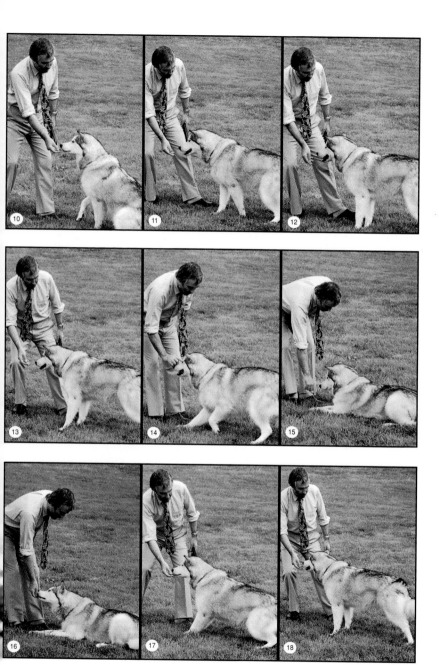

10) "Phoenix, stand!" 11) Move lure away from dog at nose height, then lower it a tad. 12) "Phoenix, off! Good stand, Phoenix!" 13) "Phoenix, down!" 14) Hand palm downwards, move lure down to lie between dog's forepaws. 15) "Phoenix, off! Good down-stay, Phoenix!" 16) "Phoenix, stand!" 17) Move lure away from dog's muzzle up to nose height. 18) "Phoenix, off! Good stand-stay, Phoenix. Now we'll make the vet and groomer happy!"

as the dog stands, lower the lure to just beneath the dog's chin to entice her to look down; otherwise she will stand and then sit immediately. To prompt the dog to stand from the down position, move the lure half a dog-length upwards and away from the dog, holding the lure at standing nose height from the floor.

Teaching **rollover** is best started from the down position, with the dog lying on one side, or at least with both hind legs stretched out on the same side. Say "Tina, bang!" and move the lure backwards and alongside the dog's muzzle to her elbow (on the side of her outstretched hind legs). Once the dog looks to the side and backwards, very slowly move the lure upwards to the dog's shoulder and backbone. Tickling the dog in the goolies (groin area) often invokes a reflex-raising of the hind leg as an appeasement gesture, which facilitates the tendency to roll over. If you move the lure too quickly and the dog jumps into the standing position, have patience and start again. As soon as the dog rolls onto her back, keep the lure stationary and mesmerize the dog with a relaxing tummy rub.

To teach **rollover-stay** when the dog is standing or moving, say "Tina, bang!" and give the appropriate hand signal (with index finger pointed and thumb cocked in true Sam Spade fashion), then in one fluid movement lure her to first lie down and then rollover-stay as above.

Teaching the dog to **stay** in each of the above four positions becomes a piece of cake after first teaching the dog not to worry at the toy or treat training lure. This is best accomplished by hand feeding dinner kibble. Hold a piece of kibble firmly in your hand and softly instruct "Off!" Ignore any licking and slobbering *for however long the dog worries at the treat*, but say "Take it!" and offer the kibble *the instant* the dog breaks contact with her muzzle. Repeat this a few times, and then up the ante and insist the dog remove her muzzle for one whole second before offering the kibble. Then progressively refine your criteria and have the dog not touch your hand (or treat) for longer and longer periods on each trial, such as for two seconds, four seconds, then six, ten, fifteen, twenty, thirty seconds and so on.

The dog soon learns: (1) worrying at the treat never gets results, whereas (2) noncontact is often rewarded after a variable time lapse.

Teaching *"Off!"* has many useful applications in its own right. Additionally, instructing the dog not to touch a training lure often produces spontaneous and magical stays. Request the dog to stand-stay, for example, and not to touch the lure. At first set your sights on a short two-second stay before rewarding the dog. (Remember, every long journey begins with a single step.) However, on subsequent trials, gradually and progressively increase the length of stay required to receive a reward. In no time at all your dog will stand calmly for a minute or so.

Relevancy Training

Once you have taught the dog what you expect her to do when requested to come, sit, lie down, stand, roll-over and stay, the time is right to teach the dog *why* she should comply with your wishes. The secret is to have many (*many*) extremely short training interludes (two to five seconds each) at numerous (*numerous*) times during the course of the dog's day. Especially work with the dog immediately *before* the dog's good times and *during* the dog's good times. For example, ask your dog to sit and/or lie down each time before opening doors, serving meals, offering treats and tummy rubs; ask the dog to perform a few controlled doggy push-ups before letting her off leash or throwing a tennis ball; and perhaps request the dog to sit-down-sit-stand-down-stand-rollover before inviting her to cuddle on the couch.

Similarly, request the dog to sit many times during play or on walks, and in no time at all the dog will be only too pleased to follow your instructions because she has learned that a compliant response heralds all sorts of goodies. Basically all you are trying to teach the dog is how to say please: "Please throw the tennis ball. Please may I snuggle on the couch."

Remember, it is important to keep training interludes short and to have many short sessions each and every day. The shortest (and most useful) session comprises asking the dog to sit and then go play during a play session. When trained this way, your dog will soon associate training with good times. In fact, the dog may be unable to distinguish between training and good times and, indeed, there should be no distinction. The warped concept that training involves forcing the dog to comply and/or dominating her will is totally at odds with the picture of a truly well-trained dog. In reality, enjoying a game of training with a dog is no different from enjoying a game of backgammon or tennis with a friend; and walking with a dog should be no different from strolling with a spouse, or with buddies on the golf course.

Walk by Your Side

Many people attempt to teach a dog to heel by putting her on a leash and physically correcting the dog when she makes mistakes. There are a number of things seriously wrong with this approach, the first being that most people do not want precision heeling; rather, they simply want the dog to follow or walk by their side. Second, when physically restrained during "training," even though the dog may grudgingly mope by your side when "handcuffed" on leash, let's see what happens when she is off leash. History! The dog is in the next county because she never enjoyed walking with you on leash and you have no control over her off leash. So let's just teach the dog off leash from the outset to *want* to walk with us. Third, if the dog has not been trained to heel, it is a trifle hasty to think about punishing the poor dog for making mistakes and breaking heeling rules she didn't even know existed. This is simply not fair! Surely, if the dog had been adequately taught how to heel, she would seldom make mistakes and hence there would be no need to correct the dog. Remember, each mistake and each correction (punishment) advertise the trainer's inadequacy, not the dog's. The dog is not stubborn, she is not stupid and she is not bad. Even if she were, she would still require training, so let's train her properly.

Let's teach the dog to *enjoy* following us and to *want* to walk by our side off leash. Then it will be easier to teach high-precision off-leash heeling patterns if desired. Before going on outdoor walks, it is necessary to teach the dog not to pull. Then it becomes easy to teach on-leash walking and heeling because the dog already wants to walk with you, she is familiar with the desired walking and heeling positions and she knows not to pull.

FOLLOWING

Start by training your dog to follow you. Many puppies will follow if you simply walk away from them and maybe click your fingers or chuckle. Adult dogs may require additional enticement to stimulate them to follow, such as a training lure or, at the very least, a lively trainer. To teach the dog to follow: (1) keep walking and (2) walk away from the dog. If the dog attempts to lead or lag, change pace; slow down if the dog forges too far ahead, but speed up if she lags too far behind. Say "Steady!" or "Easy!" each time before you slow down and "Quickly!" or "Hustle!" each time before you speed up, and the dog will learn to change pace on cue. If the dog lags or leads too far, or if she wanders right or left, simply walk quickly in the opposite direction and maybe even run away from the dog and hide.

Practicing is a lot of fun; you can set up a course in your home, yard or park to do this. Indoors, entice the dog to follow upstairs, into a bedroom, into the bathroom, downstairs, around the living room couch, zigzagging between dining room chairs and into the kitchen for dinner. Outdoors, get the dog to follow around park benches, trees, shrubs and along walkways and lines in the grass. (For safety outdoors, it is advisable to attach a long line on the dog, but never exert corrective tension on the line.)

Remember, following has a lot to do with attitude—*your* attitude! Most probably your dog will *not* want to follow Mr. Grumpy Troll with the personality of wilted lettuce. Lighten up—walk with a jaunty step, whistle a happy tune, sing, skip and tell jokes to your dog and she will be right there by your side.

BY YOUR SIDE

It is smart to train the dog to walk close on one side or the other—either side will do, your choice. When walking, jogging or cycling, it is generally bad news to have the dog suddenly cut in front of you. In fact, I train my dogs to walk "By my side" and "Other side"—both very useful instructions. It is possible to position the dog fairly accurately by looking to the appropriate side and clicking your fingers or slapping your thigh on that side. A precise positioning may be attained by holding a training lure, such as a chew toy, tennis ball or food treat. Stop and stand still several times throughout the walk, just as you would when window shopping or meeting a friend. Use the lure to make sure the dog slows down and stays close whenever you stop.

When teaching the dog to heel, we generally want her to sit in heel position when we stop. Teach heel

Using a toy to teach sit-heel-sit sequences: 1) "Phoenix, sit!" Standing still, move lure up and back over dog's muzzle . . . 2) to position dog sitting in heel position on your left side. 3) Say "Phoenix, heel!" and walk ahead, wagging lure in left hand. Change lure to right hand in preparation for sit signal. Say "Sit" and then . . .

position at the standstill and the dog will learn that the default heel position is sitting by your side (left or right—your choice, unless you wish to compete in obedience trials, in which case the dog must heel on the left).

Several times a day, stand up and call your dog to come and sit in heel position—"Tina, heel!" For example, instruct the dog to come to heel each time there are commercials on TV, or each time you turn a page of a novel, and the dog will get it in a single evening.

Practice straight-line heeling and turns separately. With the dog sitting at heel, teach her to turn in place. After each quarter-turn, half-turn or full turn in place, lure the dog to sit at heel. Now it's time for short straight-line heeling sequences, no more than a few steps at a time. Always think of heeling in terms of sit-heel-sit sequences—start and end with the dog in position and do your best to keep her there when moving. Progressively increase the number of steps in each sequence. When the dog remains close for 20 yards of straight-line heeling, it is time to add a few turns and then sign up for a happy-heeling obedience class to get some advice from the experts.

4) use hand signal to lure dog to sit as you stop. Eventually, dog will sit automatically at heel whenever you stop. 5) "Good dog!"

No Pulling on Leash

You can start teaching your dog not to pull on leash anywhere—in front of the television or outdoors—but regardless of location, you must not take a single step with tension in the leash. For a reason known only to dogs, even just a couple of paces of pulling on leash is intrinsically motivating and diabolically rewarding. Instead, attach the leash to the dog's collar, grasp the other end firmly with both hands held close to your chest, and stand still—do not budge an inch. Have somebody watch you with a stopwatch to time your progress, or else you will never believe this will work and so you will not even try the exercise, and your shoulder and the dog's neck will be traumatized for years to come.

Stand still and wait for the dog to stop pulling, and to sit and/or lie down. All dogs stop pulling and sit eventually. Most take only a couple of minutes; the all-time record is 22½ minutes. Time how long it takes. Gently praise the dog when she stops pulling, and as soon as she sits, enthusiastically praise the dog and take just one step forward, then immediately stand still. This single step usually demonstrates the ballistic reinforcing nature of pulling on leash; most dogs explode to the end of the leash, so be prepared for the strain. Stand firm and wait for the dog to sit again. Repeat this half a dozen times and you will probably notice a progressive reduction in the force of the dog's one-step explosions and a radical reduction in the time it takes for the dog to sit each time.

As the dog learns "Sit we go" and "Pull we stop," she will begin to walk forward calmly with each single step and automatically sit when you stop. Now try two steps before you stop. Wooooooo! Scary! When the dog has mastered two steps at a time, try for three. After each success, progressively increase the number of steps in the sequence: try four steps and then six, eight, ten and twenty steps before stopping. Congratulations! You are now walking the dog on leash.

Whenever walking with the dog (off leash or on leash), make sure you stop periodically to practice a few position commands and stays before instructing the dog to "Walk on!" (Remember, you want the dog to be compliant everywhere, not just in the kitchen when her dinner is at hand.) For example, stopping every 25 yards to briefly train the dog amounts to over 200 training interludes within a single 3-mile stroll. And each training session is in a different location. You will not believe the improvement within just the first mile of the first walk.

To put it another way, integrating training into a walk offers 200 separate opportunities to use the continuance of the walk as a reward to reinforce the dog's education. Moreover, some training interludes may comprise continuing education for the dog's walking skills: Alternate short periods of the dog walking calmly by your side with periods when the dog is allowed to sniff and investigate the environment. Now sniffing odors on the grass and meeting other dogs become rewards which reinforce the dog's calm and mannerly demeanor. Good Lord! Whatever next? Many enjoyable walks together of course. Happy trails!

THE IMPORTANCE OF TRICKS

Nothing will improve a dog's quality of life better than having a few tricks under her belt. Teaching any trick expands the dog's vocabulary, which facilitates communication and improves the owner's control. Also, specific tricks help prevent and resolve specific behavior problems. For example, by teaching the dog to fetch her toys, the dog learns carrying a toy makes the owner happy and, therefore, will be more likely to chew her toy than other inappropriate items.

More important, teaching tricks prompts owners to lighten up and train with a sunny disposition. Really, tricks should be no different from any other behaviors we put on cue. But they are. When teaching tricks, owners have a much sweeter attitude, which in turn motivates the dog and improves her willingness to comply. The dog feels tricks are a blast, but formal commands are a drag. In fact, tricks are so enjoyable, they may be used as rewards in training by asking the dog to come, sit and down-stay and then rollover for a tummy rub. Go on, try it: Crack a smile and even giggle when the dog promptly and willingly lies down and stays.

Most important, performing tricks prompts onlookers to smile and giggle. Many people are scared of dogs, especially large ones. And nothing can be more off-putting for a dog than to be constantly confronted by strangers who don't like her because of her size or the way she looks. Uneasy people put the dog on edge, causing her to back off and bark, only frightening people all the more. And so a vicious circle develops, with the people's fear fueling the dog's fear *and vice versa*. Instead, tie a pink ribbon to your dog's collar and practice all sorts of tricks on walks and in the park, and you will be pleasantly amazed how it changes people's attitudes toward your friendly dog. The dog's repertoire of tricks is limited only by the trainer's imagination. Below I have described three of my favorites:

SPEAK AND SHUSH

The training sequence involved in teaching a dog to bark on request is no different from that used when training any behavior on cue: request—lure—response—reward. As always, the secret of success lies in finding an effective lure. If the dog always barks at the doorbell, for example, say "Rover, speak!", have an accomplice ring the doorbell, then reward the dog for barking. After a few woofs, ask Rover to "Shush!", waggle a food treat under her nose (to entice her to sniff and thus to shush), praise her when quiet and eventually offer the treat as a reward. Alternate "Speak" and "Shush," progressively increasing the length of shush-time between each barking bout.

PLAY BOW

With the dog standing, say "Bow!" and lower the food lure (palm upwards) to rest between the dog's forepaws. Praise as the dog lowers her forequarters and sternum to the ground (as when teaching the down), but then lure the dog to stand and offer the treat. On successive trials, gradually increase the length of time the dog is required to remain in the play bow posture in order to gain a food reward. If the dog's rear end collapses into a down, say nothing and offer no reward; simply start over.

BE A BEAR

With the dog sitting backed into a corner to prevent her from toppling over backwards, say "Be a bear!" With bent paw and palm down, raise a lure upwards and backwards along the top of the dog's muzzle. Praise the dog when she sits up on her haunches and offer the treat as a reward. To prevent the dog from standing on her hind legs, keep the lure closer to the dog's muzzle. On each trial, progressively increase the length of time the dog is required to sit up to receive a food reward. Since lure-reward training is so easy, teach the dog to stand and walk on her hind legs as well!

Teaching "Be a Bear"

chapter 9

Getting
Active
with your Dog

by Bardi McLennan

Once you and your dog have graduated from basic obedience training and are beginning to work together as a team, you can take part in the growing world of dog activities. There are so many fun things to do with your dog! Just remember, people and dogs don't always learn at the same pace, so don't be upset if you (or your dog) need more than two basic training courses before your team becomes operational. Even smart dogs don't go straight to college from kindergarten!

Just as there are events geared to certain types of dogs, so there are ones that are more appealing to certain types of people. In some activities, you give the commands and your dog does the work (upland game hunting is one example), while in others, such as agility, you'll both get a workout. You may want to aim for prestigious titles to add to your dog's name, or you may want nothing more than the sheer enjoyment of being around other people and their dogs. Passive or active, participation has its own rewards.

Consider your dog's physical capabilities when looking into any of the canine activities. It's easy to see that a Basset Hound is not built for the racetrack, nor would a Chihuahua be the breed of choice for pulling a sled. A loyal dog will attempt almost anything you ask him to do, so it is up to you to know your dog's limitations. A dog must be physically sound in order to compete at any level in athletic activities, and being mentally sound is a definite plus. Advanced age, however, may not be a deterrent. Many dogs still hunt and herd at ten or twelve years of age. It's entirely possible for dogs to be "fit at 50." Take your dog for a checkup, explain to your vet the type of activity you have in mind and be guided by his or her findings.

All dogs seem to love playing flyball.

You needn't be restricted to breed-specific sports if it's only fun you're after. Certain AKC activities are limited to designated breeds; however, as each new trial, test or sport has grown in popularity, so has the variety of breeds encouraged to participate at a fun level.

But don't shortchange your fun, or that of your dog, by thinking only of the basic function of her breed. Once a dog has learned how to learn, she can be taught to do just about anything as long as the size of the dog is right for the job and you both think it is fun and rewarding. In other words, you are a team.

To get involved in any of the activities detailed in this chapter, look for the names and addresses of the organizations that sponsor them in Chapter 13. You can also ask your breeder or a local dog trainer for contacts.

You can compete in obedience trials with a well trained dog.

Official American Kennel Club Activities

The following tests and trials are some of the events sanctioned by the AKC and sponsored by various dog clubs. Your dog's expertise will be rewarded with impressive titles. You can participate just for fun, or be competitive and go for those awards.

OBEDIENCE

Training classes begin with pups as young as three months of age in kindergarten puppy training, then advance to pre-novice (all exercises on lead) and go on to novice, which is where you'll start off-lead work. In obedience classes dogs learn to sit, stay, heel and come through a variety of exercises. Once you've got the basics down, you can enter obedience trials and work toward earning your dog's first degree, a C.D. (Companion Dog).

The next level is called "Open," in which jumps and retrieves perk up the dog's interest. Passing grades in competition at this level earn a C.D.X. (Companion Dog Excellent). Beyond that lies the goal of the most ambitious—Utility (U.D. and even U.D.X. or OTCh, an Obedience Champion).

AGILITY

All dogs can participate in the latest canine sport to have gained worldwide popularity for its fun and excitement, agility. It began in England as a canine version of horse show-jumping, but because dogs are more agile and able to perform on verbal commands, extra feats were added such as climbing, balancing and racing through tunnels or in and out of weave poles. Many of the obstacles (regulation or homemade) can be set up in your own backyard. If the agility bug bites, you could end up in international competition!

For starters, your dog should be obedience trained, even though, in the beginning, the lessons may all be taught on lead. Once the dog understands the commands (and you do, too), it's as easy as guiding the dog over a prescribed course, one obstacle at a time. In competition, the race is against the clock, so wear your running shoes! The dog starts with 200 points and the judge deducts for infractions and misadventures along the way.

All dogs seem to love agility and respond to it as if they were being turned loose in a playground paradise. Your dog's enthusiasm will be contagious; agility turns into great fun for dog and owner.

FIELD TRIALS AND HUNTING TESTS

There are field trials and hunting tests for the sporting breeds—retrievers, spaniels and pointing breeds, and for some hounds—Bassets, Beagles and Dachshunds. Field trials are competitive events that test a dog's ability to perform the functions for which she was bred. Hunting tests, which are open to retrievers,

---

TITLES AWARDED BY THE AKC

Conformation: Ch. (Champion)

Obedience: CD (Companion Dog); CDX (Companion Dog Excellent); UD (Utility Dog); UDX (Utility Dog Excellent); OTCh. (Obedience Trial Champion)

Field: JH (Junior Hunter); SH (Senior Hunter); MH (Master Hunter); AFCh. (Amateur Field Champion); FCh. (Field Champion)

Lure Coursing: JC (Junior Courser); SC (Senior Courser)

Herding: HT (Herding Tested); PT (Pre-Trial Tested); HS (Herding Started); HI (Herding Intermediate); HX (Herding Excellent); HCh. (Herding Champion)

Tracking: TD (Tracking Dog); TDX (Tracking Dog Excellent)

Agility: NAD (Novice Agility); OAD (Open Agility); ADX (Agility Excellent); MAX (Master Agility)

Earthdog Tests: JE (Junior Earthdog); SE (Senior Earthdog); ME (Master Earthdog)

Canine Good Citizen: CGC

Combination: DC (Dual Champion—Ch. and FCh.); TC (Triple Champion—Ch., FCh., and OTCh.)

---

spaniels and pointing breeds only, are noncompetitive
and are a means of judging the dog's ability as well as
that of the handler.

Hunting is a very large and complex part of canine
sports, and if you own one of the breeds that hunts, the
events are a great treat for your dog and you. He gets
to do what he was bred for, and you get to work with
him and watch him do it. You'll be proud of and
amazed at what your dog can do.

Fortunately, the AKC publishes a series of booklets on
these events, which outline the rules and regulations
and include a glossary of the sometimes complicated
terms. The AKC also publishes newsletters for field tri-
alers and hunting test enthusiasts. The United Kennel
Club (UKC) also has informative materials for the
hunter and his dog.

*Retrievers and
other sporting
breeds get to do
what they're
bred to in hunt-
ing tests.*

HERDING TESTS AND TRIALS

Herding, like hunting, dates
back to the first known uses man
made of dogs. The interest in
herding today is widespread,
and if you own a herding breed,
you can join in the activity.
Herding dogs are tested for
their natural skills to keep a
flock of ducks, sheep or cattle
together. If your dog shows
potential, you can start at the
testing level, where your dog can
earn a title for showing an inherent herding ability.
With training you can advance to the trial level, where
your dog should be capable of controlling even difficult livestock in diverse situations.

LURE COURSING

The AKC Tests and Trials for Lure Coursing are open
to traditional sighthounds—Greyhounds, Whippets,

Borzoi, Salukis, Afghan Hounds, Ibizan Hounds and Scottish Deerhounds—as well as to Basenjis and Rhodesian Ridgebacks. Hounds are judged on overall ability, follow, speed, agility and endurance. This is possibly the most exciting of the trials for spectators, because the speed and agility of the dogs is awesome to watch as they chase the lure (or "course") in heats of two or three dogs at a time.

TRACKING

Tracking is another activity in which almost any dog can compete because every dog that sniffs the ground when taken outdoors is, in fact, tracking. The hard part comes when the rules as to what, when and where the dog tracks are determined by a person, not the dog! Tracking tests cover a large area of fields, woods and roads. The tracks are laid hours before the dogs go to work on them, and include "tricks" like cross-tracks and sharp turns. If you're interested in search-and-rescue work, this is the place to start.

This tracking dog is hot on the trail.

EARTHDOG TESTS FOR SMALL TERRIERS AND DACHSHUNDS

These tests are open to Australian, Bedlington, Border, Cairn, Dandie Dinmont, Smooth and Wire Fox, Lakeland, Norfolk, Norwich, Scottish, Sealyham, Skye, Welsh and West Highland White Terriers as well as Dachshunds. The dogs need no prior training for this terrier sport. There is a qualifying test on the day of the event, so dog and handler learn the rules on the spot. These tests, or "digs," sometimes end with informal races in the late afternoon.

Here are some of the extracurricular obedience and racing activities that are not regulated by the AKC or UKC, but are generally run by clubs or a group of dog fanciers and are often open to all.

Canine Freestyle This activity is something new on the scene and is variously likened to dancing, dressage or ice skating. It is meant to show the athleticism of the dog, but also requires showmanship on the part of the dog's handler. If you and your dog like to ham it up for friends, you might want to look into freestyle.

Lure coursing lets sighthounds do what they do best—run!

Scent Hurdle Racing Scent hurdle racing is purely a fun activity sponsored by obedience clubs with members forming competing teams. The height of the hurdles is based on the size of the shortest dog on the team. On a signal, one team dog is released on each of two side-by-side courses and must clear every hurdle before picking up its own dumbbell from a platform and returning over the jumps to the handler. As each dog returns, the next on that team is sent. Of course, that is what the dogs are supposed to do. When the dogs improvise (going under or around the hurdles, stealing another dog's dumbbell, and so forth), it no doubt frustrates the handlers, but just adds to the fun for everyone else.

Flyball This type of racing is similar, but after negotiating the four hurdles, the dog comes to a flyball box, steps on a lever that releases a tennis ball into the air, catches the ball and returns over the hurdles to the starting point. This game also becomes extremely fun for spectators because the dogs sometimes cheat by catching a ball released by the dog in the next lane. Three titles can be earned—Flyball Dog (F.D.), Flyball Dog Excellent (F.D.X.) and Flyball Dog Champion (Fb.D.Ch.)—all awarded by the North American Flyball Association, Inc.

Dogsledding The name conjures up the Rocky Mountains or the frigid North, but you can find dogsled clubs in such unlikely spots as Maryland, North Carolina and Virginia! Dogsledding is primarily for the Nordic breeds such as the Alaskan Malamutes, Siberian Huskies and Samoyeds, but other breeds can try. There are some practical backyard applications to this sport, too. With parental supervision, almost any strong dog could pull a child's sled.

Coming over the A-frame on an agility course.

These are just some of the many recreational ways you can get to know and understand your multifaceted dog better and have fun doing it.

chapter 10

Your Dog
and your
Family

by Bardi McLennan

Adding a dog automatically increases your family by one, no matter whether you live alone in an apartment or are part of a mother, father and six kids household. The single-person family is fair game for numerous and varied canine misconceptions as to who is dog and who pays the bills, whereas a dog in a houseful of children will consider himself to be just one of the gang, littermates all. One dog and one child may give a dog reason to believe they are both kids or both dogs. Either interpretation requires parental supervision and sometimes speedy intervention.

As soon as one paw goes through the door into your home, Rufus (or Rufina) has to make many adjustments to become a part of your

136

family. Your job is to make him fit in as painlessly as possible. An older dog may have some frame of reference from past experience, but to a 10-week-old puppy, everything is brand new: people, furniture, stairs, when and where people eat, sleep or watch TV, his own place and everyone else's space, smells, sounds, out-doors—everything!

Puppies, and newly acquired dogs of any age, do not need what we think of as "freedom." If you leave a new dog or puppy loose in the house, you will almost certainly return to chaotic destruction and the dog will forever after equate your homecoming with a time of punishment to be dreaded. It is unfair to give your dog what amounts to "freedom to get into trouble." Instead, confine him to a crate for brief periods of your absence (up to three or four hours) and, for the long haul, a workday for example, confine him to one untrashable area with his own toys, a bowl of water and a radio left on (low) in another room.

Lots of pets get along with each other just fine.

For the first few days, when not confined, put Rufus on a long leash tied to your wrist or waist. This umbilical cord method enables the dog to learn all about you from your body language and voice, and to learn by his own actions which things in the house are NO! and which ones are rewarded by "Good dog." House-training will be easier with the pup always by your side. Speaking of which, accidents do happen. That goal of "completely housetrained" takes up to a year, or the length of time it takes the pup to mature.

The All-Adult Family

Most dogs in an adults-only household today are likely to be latchkey pets, with no one home all day but the dog. When you return after a tough day on the job, the dog can and should be your relaxation therapy. But going home can instead be a daily frustration.

Separation anxiety is a very common problem for the dog in a working household. It may begin with whines and barks of loneliness, but it will soon escalate into a frenzied destruction derby. That is why it is so important to set aside the time to teach a dog to relax when left alone in his confined area and to understand that he can trust you to return.

Let the dog get used to your work schedule in easy stages. Confine him to one room and go in and out of that room over and over again. Be casual about it. No physical, voice or eye contact. When the pup no longer even notices your comings and goings, leave the house for varying lengths of time, returning to stay home for a few minutes and gradually increasing the time away. This training can take days, but the dog is learning that you haven't left him forever and that he can trust you.

Any time you leave the dog, but especially during this training period, be casual about your departure. No anxiety-building fond farewells. Just "Bye" and go! Remember the "Good dog" when you return to find everything more or less as you left it.

If things are a mess (or even a disaster) when you return, greet the dog, take him outside to eliminate, and then put him in his crate while you clean up. Rant and rave in the shower! *Do not* punish the dog. You were not there when it happened, and the rule is: Only punish as you catch the dog in the act of wrongdoing. Obviously, it makes sense to get your latchkey puppy when you'll have a week or two to spend on these training essentials.

Family weekend activities should include Rufus whenever possible. Depending on the pup's age, now is the time for a long walk in the park, playtime in the backyard, a hike in the woods. Socializing is as important as health care, good food and physical exercise, so visiting Aunt Emma or Uncle Harry and the next-door neighbor's dog or cat is essential to developing an outgoing, friendly temperament in your pet.

If you are a single adult, socializing Rufus at home and away will prevent him from becoming overly protective of you (or just overly attached) and will also prevent such behavioral problems as dominance or fear of strangers.

Babies

Whether already here or on the way, babies figure larger than life in the eyes of a dog. If the dog is there first, let him in on all your baby preparations in the house. When baby arrives, let Rufus sniff any item of clothing that has been on the baby before Junior comes home. Then let Mom greet the dog first before introducing the new family member. Hold the baby down for the dog to see and sniff, but make sure someone's holding the dog on lead in case of any sudden moves. Don't play keep-away or tease the dog with the baby, which only invites undesirable jumping up.

The dog and the baby are "family," and for starters can be treated almost as equals. Things rapidly change, however, especially when baby takes to creeping around on all fours on the dog's turf or, better yet, has yummy pudding all over her face and hands! That's when a lot of things in the dog's and baby's lives become more separate than equal.

Dogs are perfect confidants.

Toddlers make terrible dog owners, but if you can't avoid the combination, use patient discipline (that is, positive teaching rather than punishment), and use time-outs before you run out of patience.

A dog and a baby (or toddler, or an assertive young child) should never be left alone together. Take the dog with you or confine him. With a baby or youngsters in the house, you'll have plenty of use for that wonderful canine safety device called a crate!

Young Children

Any dog in a house with kids will behave pretty much as the kids do, good or bad. But even good dogs and good children can get into trouble when play becomes rowdy and active.

Teach children how to play nicely with a puppy.

Legs bobbing up and down, shrill voices screeching, a ball hurtling overhead, all add up to exuberant frustration for a dog who's just trying to be part of the gang. In a pack of puppies, any legs or toys being chased would be caught by a set of teeth, and all the pups involved would understand that is how the game is played. Kids do not understand this, nor do parents tolerate it. Bring Rufus indoors before you have reason to regret it. This is time-out, not a punishment.

You can explain the situation to the children and tell them they must play quieter games until the puppy learns not to grab them with his mouth. Unfortunately, you can't explain it that easily to the dog. With adult supervision, they will learn how to play together.

Young children love to tease. Sticking their faces or wiggling their hands or fingers in the dog's face is teasing. To another person it might be just annoying, but it is threatening to a dog. There's another difference: We can make the child stop by an explanation, but the only way a dog can stop it is with a warning growl and then with teeth. Teasing is the major cause of children being bitten by their pets. Treat it seriously.

140

Older Children

The best age for a child to get a first dog is between the ages of 8 and 12. That's when kids are able to accept some real responsibility for their pet. Even so, take the child's vow of "I will never *ever* forget to feed (brush, walk, etc.) the dog" for what it's worth: a child's good intention at that moment. Most kids today have extra lessons, soccer practice, Little League, ballet, and so forth piled on top of school schedules. There will be many times when Mom will have to come to the dog's rescue. "I walked the dog for you so you can set the table for me" is one way to get around a missed appointment without laying on blame or guilt.

Kids in this age group make excellent obedience trainers because they are into the teaching/learning process themselves and they lack the self-consciousness of adults. Attending a dog show is something the whole family can enjoy, and watching Junior Showmanship may catch the eye of the kids. Older children can begin to get involved in many of the recreational activities that were reviewed in the previous chapter. Some of the agility obstacles, for example, can be set up in the backyard as a family project (with an adult making sure all the equipment is safe and secure for the dog).

Older kids are also beginning to look to the future, and may envision themselves as veterinarians or trainers or show dog handlers or writers of the next Lassie best-seller. Dogs are perfect confidants for these dreams. They won't tell a soul.

Other Pets

Introduce all pets tactfully. In a dog/cat situation, hold the dog, not the cat. Let two dogs meet on neutral turf—a stroll in the park or a walk down the street—with both on loose leads to permit all the normal canine ways of saying hello, including routine sniffing, circling, more sniffing, and so on. Small creatures such as hamsters, chinchillas or mice must be kept safe from their natural predators (dogs and cats).

Festive Family Occasions

Parties are great for people, but not necessarily for puppies. Until all the guests have arrived, put the dog in his crate or in a room where he won't be disturbed. A socialized dog can join the fun later as long as he's not underfoot, annoying guests or into the hors d'oeuvres.

There are a few dangers to consider, too. Doors opening and closing can allow a puppy to slip out unnoticed in the confusion, and you'll be organizing a search party instead of playing host or hostess. Party food and buffet service are not for dogs. Let Rufus party in his crate with a nice big dog biscuit.

At Christmas time, not only are tree decorations dangerous and breakable (and perhaps family heirlooms), but extreme caution should be taken with the lights, cords and outlets for the tree lights and any other festive lighting. Occasionally a dog lifts a leg, ignoring the fact that the tree is indoors. To avoid this, use a canine repellent, made for gardens, on the tree. Or keep him out of the tree room unless supervised. And whatever you do, *don't* invite trouble by hanging his toys on the tree!

Car Travel

Before you plan a vacation by car or RV with Rufus, be sure he enjoys car travel. Nothing spoils a holiday quicker than a carsick dog! Work within the dog's comfort level. Get in the car with the dog in his crate or attached to a canine car safety belt and just sit there until he relaxes. That's all. Next time, get in the car, turn on the engine and go nowhere. Just sit. When that is okay, turn on the engine and go around the block. Now you can go for a ride and include a stop where you get out, leaving the dog for a minute or two.

On a warm day, always park in the shade and leave windows open several inches. And return quickly. It only takes 10 minutes for a car to become an overheated steel death trap.

Motel or Pet Motel?

Not all motels or hotels accept pets, but you have a much better choice today than even a few years ago. To find a dog-friendly lodging, look at *On the Road Again With Man's Best Friend*, a series of directories that detail bed and breakfasts, inns, family resorts and other hotels/motels. Some places require a refundable deposit to cover any damage incurred by the dog. More B&Bs accept pets now, but some restrict the size.

If taking Rufus with you is not feasible, check out boarding kennels in your area. Your veterinarian may offer this service, or recommend a kennel or two he or she is familiar with. Go see the facilities for yourself, ask about exercise, diet, housing, and so on. Or, if you'd rather have Rufus stay home, look into bonded petsitters, many of whom will also bring in the mail and water your plants.

chapter 11

Your Dog
and your
Community

by Bardi McLennan

Step outside your home with your dog and you are no longer just family, you are both part of your community. This is when the phrase "responsible pet ownership" takes on serious implications. For starters, it means you pick up after your dog—not just occasionally, but every time your dog eliminates away from home. That means you have joined the Plastic Baggy Brigade! You always have plastic sandwich bags in your pocket and several in the car. It means you teach your kids how to use them, too. If you think this is "yucky," just imagine what

the person (a non-doggy person) who inadvertently steps in the mess thinks!

144

Your responsibility extends to your neighbors: To their ears (no annoying barking); to their property (their garbage, their lawn, their flower beds, their cat—especially their cat); to their kids (on bikes, at play); to their kids' toys and sports equipment.

There are numerous dog-related laws, ranging from simple dog licensing and leash laws to those holding you liable for any physical injury or property damage done by your dog. These laws are in place to protect everyone in the community, including you and your dog. There are town ordinances and state laws which are by no means the same in all towns or all states. Ignorance of the law won't get you off the hook. The time to find out what the laws are where you live is now.

Be sure your dog's license is current. This is not just a good local ordinance, it can make the difference between finding your lost dog or not. Many states now require proof of rabies vaccination and that the dog has been spayed or neutered before issuing a license. At the same time, keep up the dog's annual immunizations.

Dressing your dog up makes him appealing to strangers.

Never let your dog run loose in the neighborhood. This will not only keep you on the right side of the leash law, it's the outdoor version of the rule about not giving your dog "freedom to get into trouble."

Good Canine Citizen

Sometimes it's hard for a dog's owner to assess whether or not the dog is sufficiently socialized to be accepted by the community at large. Does Rufus or Rufina display good, controlled behavior in public? The AKC's Canine Good Citizen program is available through many dog organizations. If your dog passes the test, the title "CGC" is earned.

The overall purpose is to turn your dog into a good neighbor and to teach you about your responsibility to your community as a dog owner. Here are the ten things your dog must do willingly:

1. Accept a stranger stopping to chat with you.
2. Sit and be petted by a stranger.
3. Allow a stranger to handle him or her as a groomer or veterinarian would.
4. Walk nicely on a loose lead.
5. Walk calmly through a crowd.
6. Sit and down on command, then stay in a sit or down position while you walk away.
7. Come when called.
8. Casually greet another dog.
9. React confidently to distractions.
10. Accept being left alone with someone other than you and not become overly agitated or nervous.

Schools and Dogs

Schools are getting involved with pet ownership on an educational level. It has been proven that children who are kind to animals are humane in their attitude toward other people as adults.

A dog is a child's best friend, and so children are often primary pet owners, if not the primary caregivers. Unfortunately, they are also the ones most often bitten by dogs. This occurs due to a lack of understanding that pets, no matter how sweet, cuddly and loving, are still animals. Schools, along with parents, dog clubs, dog fanciers and the AKC, are working to change all that with video programs for children not only in grade school, but in the nursery school and pre-kindergarten age group. Teaching youngsters how to be responsible dog owners is important community work. When your dog has a CGC, volunteer to take part in an educational classroom event put on by your dog club.

Boy Scout Merit Badge

A Merit Badge for Dog Care can be earned by any Boy Scout ages 11 to 18. The requirements are not easy, but amount to a complete course in responsible dog care and general ownership. Here are just a few of the things a Scout must do to earn that badge:

Point out ten parts of the dog using the correct names.

Give a report (signed by parent or guardian) on your care of the dog (feeding, food used, housing, exercising, grooming and bathing), plus what has been done to keep the dog healthy.

Explain the right way to obedience train a dog, and demonstrate three comments.

Several of the requirements have to do with health care, including first aid, handling a hurt dog, and the dangers of home treatment for a serious ailment.

The final requirement is to know the local laws and ordinances involving dogs.

There are similar programs for Girl Scouts and 4-H members.

Local Clubs

Local dog clubs are no longer in existence just to put on a yearly dog show. Today, they are apt to be the hub of the community's involvement with pets. Dog clubs conduct educational forums with big-name speakers, stage demonstrations of canine talent in a busy mall and take dogs of various breeds to schools for class-room discussion.

The quickest way to feel accepted as a member in a club is to volunteer your services! Offer to help with something—anything—and watch your popularity (and your interest) grow.

Therapy Dogs

Once your dog has earned that essential CGC and reliably demonstrates a steady, calm temperament, you could look into what therapy dogs are doing in your area.

Therapy dogs go with their owners to visit patients at hospitals or nursing homes, generally remaining on leash but able to coax a pat from a stiffened hand, a smile from a blank face, a few words from sealed lips or a hug from someone in need of love.

Nursing homes cover a wide range of patient care. Some specialize in care of the elderly, some in the treatment of specific illnesses, some in physical therapy. Children's facilities also welcome visits from trained therapy dogs for boosting morale in their pediatric patients. Hospice care for the terminally ill and the at-home care of AIDS patients are other areas where this canine visiting is desperately needed. Therapy dog training comes first.

Your dog can make a differ-ence in lots of lives.

There is a lot more involved than just taking your nice friendly pooch to someone's bedside. Doing therapy dog work involves your own emotional stability as well as that of your dog. But once you have met all the requirements for this work, making the rounds once a week or once a month with your therapy dog is possibly the most rewarding of all community activities.

Disaster Aid

This community service is definitely not for everyone, partly because it is time-consuming. The initial training is rigorous, and there can be no let-up in the continuing workouts, because members are on call 24 hours a day to go wherever they are needed at a moment's notice. But if you think you would like to be able to assist in a disaster, look into search-and-rescue work. The network of search-and-rescue volunteers is worldwide, and all members of the American Rescue Dog Association (ARDA) who are qualified to do this work are volunteers who train and maintain their own dogs.

Physical Aid

Most people are familiar with Seeing Eye dogs, which serve as blind people's eyes, but not with all the other work that dogs are trained to do to assist the disabled. Dogs are also specially trained to pull wheelchairs, carry school books, pick up dropped objects, open and close doors. Some also are ears for the deaf. All these assistance-trained dogs, by the way, are allowed anywhere "No Pet" signs exist (as are therapy dogs when properly identified). Getting started in any of this fascinating work requires a background in dog training and canine behavior, but there are also volunteer jobs ranging from answering the phone to cleaning out kennels to providing a foster home for a puppy. You have only to ask.

Making the rounds with your therapy dog can be very rewarding.

part four

Beyond
the

Basics

chapter 12

Recommended Reading

Books

ABOUT HEALTH CARE

Ackerman, Lowell. *Guide to Skin and Haircoat Problems in Dogs.* Loveland, Colo.: Alpine Publications, 1994.

Alderton, David. *The Dog Care Manual.* Hauppauge, N.Y.: Barron's Educational Series, Inc., 1986.

American Kennel Club. *American Kennel Club Dog Care and Training.* New York: Howell Book House, 1991.

Bamberger, Michelle, DVM. *Help! The Quick Guide to First Aid for Your Dog.* New York: Howell Book House, 1995.

Carlson, Delbert, DVM, and James Giffin, MD. *Dog Owner's Home Veterinary Handbook.* New York: Howell Book House, 1992.

DeBitetto, James, DVM, and Sarah Hodgson. *You & Your Puppy.* New York: Howell Book House, 1995.

Humphries, Jim, DVM. *Dr. Jim's Animal Clinic for Dogs.* New York: Howell Book House, 1994.

McGinnis, Terri. *The Well Dog Book.* New York: Random House, 1991.

Pitcairn, Richard and Susan. *Natural Health for Dogs.* Emmaus, Pa.: Rodale Press, 1982.

ABOUT DOG SHOWS

Hall, Lynn. *Dog Showing for Beginners.* New York: Howell Book House, 1994.

Nichols, Virginia Tuck. *How to Show Your Own Dog.* Neptune, N. J.: TFH, 1970.

Vanacore, Connie. *Dog Showing, An Owner's Guide.* New York: Howell Book House, 1990.

ABOUT TRAINING

Ammen, Amy. *Training in No Time*. New York: Howell Book House, 1995.

Baer, Ted. *Communicating With Your Dog*. Hauppauge, N.Y.: Barron's Educational Series, Inc., 1989.

Benjamin, Carol Lea. *Dog Problems*. New York: Howell Book House, 1989.

Benjamin, Carol Lea. *Dog Training for Kids*. New York: Howell Book House, 1988.

Benjamin, Carol Lea. *Mother Knows Best*. New York: Howell Book House, 1985.

Benjamin, Carol Lea. *Surviving Your Dog's Adolescence*. New York: Howell Book House, 1993.

Bohnenkamp, Gwen. *Manners for the Modern Dog*. San Francisco: Perfect Paws, 1990.

Dibra, Bashkim. *Dog Training by Bash*. New York: Dell, 1992.

Dunbar, Ian, PhD, MRCVS. *Dr. Dunbar's Good Little Dog Book*, James & Kenneth Publishers, 2140 Shattuck Ave. #2406, Berkeley, Calif. 94704. (510) 658–8588. Order from the publisher.

Dunbar, Ian, PhD, MRCVS. *How to Teach a New Dog Old Tricks*, James & Kenneth Publishers. Order from the publisher; address above.

Dunbar, Ian, PhD, MRCVS, and Gwen Bohnenkamp. Booklets on *Preventing Aggression; Housetraining; Chewing; Digging; Barking; Socialization; Fearfulness; and Fighting*, James & Kenneth Publishers. Order from the publisher; address above.

Evans, Job Michael. *People, Pooches and Problems*. New York: Howell Book House, 1991.

Kilcommons, Brian and Sarah Wilson. *Good Owners, Great Dogs*. New York: Warner Books, 1992.

McMains, Joel M. *Dog Logic—Companion Obedience*. New York: Howell Book House, 1992.

Rutherford, Clarice and David H. Neil, MRCVS. *How to Raise a Puppy You Can Live With*. Loveland, Colo.: Alpine Publications, 1982.

Volhard, Jack and Melissa Bartlett. *What All Good Dogs Should Know: The Sensible Way to Train*. New York: Howell Book House, 1991.

ABOUT BREEDING

Harris, Beth J. Finder. *Breeding a Litter, The Complete Book of Prenatal and Postnatal Care*. New York: Howell Book House, 1983.

Holst, Phyllis, DVM. *Canine Reproduction*. Loveland, Colo.: Alpine Publications, 1985.

Walkowicz, Chris and Bonnie Wilcox, DVM. *Successful Dog Breeding, The Complete Handbook of Canine Midwifery.* New York: Howell Book House, 1994.

ABOUT ACTIVITIES

American Rescue Dog Association. *Search and Rescue Dogs.* New York: Howell Book House, 1991.

Barwig, Susan and Stewart Hilliard. *Schutzhund.* New York: Howell Book House, 1991.

Beaman, Arthur S. *Lure Coursing.* New York: Howell Book House, 1994.

Daniels, Julie. *Enjoying Dog Agility—From Backyard to Competition.* New York: Doral Publishing, 1990.

Davis, Kathy Diamond. *Therapy Dogs.* New York: Howell Book House, 1992.

Gallup, Davis Anne. *Running With Man's Best Friend.* Loveland, Colo.: Alpine Publications, 1986.

Habgood, Dawn and Robert. *On the Road Again With Man's Best Friend.* New England, Mid-Atlantic, West Coast and Southeast editions. Selective guides to area bed and breakfasts, inns, hotels and resorts that welcome guests and their dogs. New York: Howell Book House, 1995.

Holland, Vergil S. *Herding Dogs.* New York: Howell Book House, 1994.

LaBelle, Charlene G. *Backpacking With Your Dog.* Loveland, Colo.: Alpine Publications, 1993.

Simmons-Moake, Jane. *Agility Training, The Fun Sport for All Dogs.* New York: Howell Book House, 1991.

Spencer, James B. *Hup! Training Flushing Spaniels the American Way.* New York: Howell Book House, 1992.

Spencer, James B. *Point! Training the All-Seasons Birddog.* New York: Howell Book House, 1995.

Tarrant, Bill. *Training the Hunting Retriever.* New York: Howell Book House, 1991.

Volhard, Jack and Wendy. *The Canine Good Citizen.* New York: Howell Book House, 1994.

General Titles

Haggerty, Captain Arthur J. *How to Get Your Pet Into Show Business.* New York: Howell Book House, 1994.

McLennan, Bardi. *Dogs and Kids, Parenting Tips.* New York: Howell Book House, 1993.

Moran, Patti J. *Pet Sitting for Profit, A Complete Manual for Professional Success.* New York: Howell Book House, 1992.

Scalisi, Danny and Libby Moses. *When Rover Just Won't Do, Over 2,000 Suggestions for Naming Your Dog.* New York: Howell Book House, 1993.

Sife, Wallace, PhD. *The Loss of a Pet.* New York: Howell Book House, 1993.

Wrede, Barbara J. *Civilizing Your Puppy.* Hauppauge, N.Y.: Barron's Educational Series, 1992.

Magazines

The AKC GAZETTE, The Official Journal for the Sport of Purebred Dogs. American Kennel Club, 51 Madison Ave., New York, NY.

Bloodlines Journal. United Kennel Club, 100 E. Kilgore Rd., Kalamazoo, MI.

Dog Fancy. Fancy Publications, 3 Burroughs, Irvine, CA 92718

Dog World. Maclean Hunter Publishing Corp., 29 N. Wacker Dr., Chicago, IL 60606.

Videos

"SIRIUS Puppy Training," by Ian Dunbar, PhD, MRCVS. James & Kenneth Publishers, 2140 Shattuck Ave. #2406, Berkeley, CA 94704. Order from the publisher.

"Training the Companion Dog," from Dr. Dunbar's British TV Series, James & Kenneth Publishers. (See address above).

The American Kennel Club produces videos on every breed of dog, as well as on hunting tests, field trials and other areas of interest to purebred dog owners. For more information, write to AKC/Video Fulfillment, 5580 Centerview Dr., Suite 200, Raleigh, NC 27606.

chapter 13

Resources

Breed Clubs

Every breed recognized by the American Kennel Club has a national (parent) club. National clubs are a great source of information on your breed. You can get the name of the secretary of the club by contacting:

The American Kennel Club
51 Madison Avenue
New York, NY 10010
(212) 696-8200

There are also numerous all-breed, individual breed, obedience, hunting and other special-interest dog clubs across the country. The American Kennel Club can provide you with a geographical list of clubs to find ones in your area. Contact them at the above address.

Registry Organizations

Registry organizations register purebred dogs. The American Kennel Club is the oldest and largest in this country, and currently recognizes over 130 breeds. The United Kennel Club registers some breeds the AKC doesn't (including the American Pit Bull Terrier and the Miniature Fox Terrier) as well as many of the same breeds. The others included here are for your reference; the AKC can provide you with a list of foreign registries.

American Kennel Club
51 Madison Avenue
New York, NY 10010

United Kennel Club (UKC)
100 E. Kilgore Road
Kalamazoo, MI 49001-5598

American Dog Breeders Assn.
P.O. Box 1771
Salt Lake City, UT 84110
(Registers American Pit Bull Terriers)

Canadian Kennel Club
89 Skyway Avenue
Etobicoke, Ontario
Canada M9W 6R4

National Stock Dog Registry
P.O. Box 402
Butler, IN 46721
(Registers working stock dogs)

Orthopedic Foundation for Animals (OFA)
2300 E. Nifong Blvd.
Columbia, MO 65201-3856
(Hip registry)

Activity Clubs

Write to these organizations for information on the
activities they sponsor.

American Kennel Club
51 Madison Avenue
New York, NY 10010
(Conformation Shows, Obedience Trials, Field
Trials and Hunting Tests, Agility, Canine Good

Citizen, Lure Coursing, Herding, Tracking,
Earthdog Tests, Coonhunting.)

United Kennel Club
100 E. Kilgore Road
Kalamazoo, MI 49001-5598
(Conformation Shows, Obedience Trials, Agility,
Hunting for Various Breeds, Terrier Trials and
more.)

North American Flyball Assn.
1342 Jeff St.
Ypsilanti, MI 48198

International Sled Dog Racing Assn.
P.O. Box 446
Norman, ID 83848-0446

North American Working Dog Assn., Inc.
Southeast Kreisgruppe
P.O. Box 833
Brunswick, GA 31521

Trainers

Association of Pet Dog Trainers
P.O. Box 385
Davis, CA 95617
(800) PET–DOGS

American Dog Trainers' Network
161 West 4th St.
New York, NY 10014
(212) 727–7257

**National Association of Dog Obedience
Instructors**
2286 East Steel Rd.
St. Johns, MI 48879

Associations

American Dog Owners Assn.
1654 Columbia Tpk.
Castleton, NY 12033
(Combats anti-dog legislation)

Delta Society
P.O. Box 1080
Renton, WA 98057-1080
(Promotes the human/animal bond through
pet-assisted therapy and other programs)

Dog Writers Assn. of America (DWAA)
Sally Cooper, Secy.
222 Woodchuck Ln.
Harwinton, CT 06791

National Assn. for Search and Rescue (NASAR)
P.O. Box 3709
Fairfax, VA 22038

Therapy Dogs International
6 Hilltop Road
Mendham, NJ 07945